Praise for
The Apocalypse of Ahmadinejad

"Too few in the West understand just how dangerous Iranian president Mahmoud Ahmadinejad really is. Few truly see him as a rising new Hitler, determined to wipe Israel off the map. Fewer still realize he's the head of an apocalyptic cult hellbent on acquiring nuclear weapons and annihilating the U.S. as well, all to usher in the Islamic messiah. But Mark Hitchcock gets it. His research is first-rate, and his book is a must-read."

—JOEL C. ROSENBERG, New York Times best-selling
author of *Epicenter*

"*The Apocalypse of Ahmadinejad* will open your eyes to the world's greatest threat to Israel and the United States, a threat that is growing stronger every day. I highly recommend Mark and this book as faithful guides to understanding current events in light of God's wonderful plan of prophecy."

—TIM LAHAYE, coauthor of the Left Behind series

THE
APOCALYPSE
OF
AHMADINEJAD

THE
APOCALYPSE
OF
AHMADINEJAD

THE REVELATION OF IRAN'S
NUCLEAR PROPHET

MARK HITCHCOCK

MULTNOMAH
BOOKS

THE APOCALYPSE OF AHMADINEJAD
PUBLISHED BY MULTNOMAH BOOKS
12265 Oracle Boulevard, Suite 200
Colorado Springs, Colorado 80921
A division of Random House Inc.

ISBN 978-1-60142-102-9

Library of Congress Cataloging-in-Publication Data

Hitchcock, Mark.
    The apocalypse of Ahmadinejad / Mark Hitchcock. — 1st ed.
        p. cm.
    Includes bibliographical references and index.
    ISBN 978-1-60142-102-9 (alk. paper)
    1. Ahmadinejad, Mahmoud. 2. Iran—Politics and government—1997–.
3. Nuclear weapons—Iran. 4. Iran—Forecasting. 5. Iran—Strategic aspects.
6. Islam and politics—Iran. I. Title.
    DS318.84.A36H58 2007
    955.06'1092—dc22

                                    2007024085

Printed in the United States of America
2007—First Edition

10 9 8 7 6 5 4 3 2 1

To Bill Jensen
Thank you for your faithful friendship,
your inspiring encouragement,
and your passion for the blessed hope.

CONTENTS

Iran is the most important geostrategic change of the 21st century.

MORTIMER ZUCKERMAN, *SCARBOROUGH COUNTRY*
(FEBRUARY 1, 2007)

Those of us trying to make sense of the Middle East remain perplexed by the recent rise of Iranian President Mahmoud Ahmadinejad, the lunatic-like leader with decidedly sociopathic tendencies. Not only will Iran soon develop a deliverable nuclear device, he promises, but the first hit will be Israel. These are the rantings of a crazy man. The only question is whether President Ahmadinejad is crazy like a fox.... Dealing with al Qaeda may turn out to have been child's play. After all, in the case of the new Iranian president, who studied traffic planning in a doctoral program, we are talking about an individual who recently wrote that the end of the world will occur in his lifetime. He's fifty years old.

DAVID SMICK, *THE INTERNATIONAL ECONOMY*
(WINTER 2006)

As a devout Shiite Muslim, Iranian President Mahmoud Ahmadinejad is telling colleagues in Tehran that he believes the end of the world is rapidly approaching. He also believes that the way to hasten the coming of the Islamic Messiah known as the "Hidden Imam" or the "Mahdi" is to launch a catastrophic global jihad, first against Israel (the "little Satan") and then against the U.S. (the "Great Satan"). What's more, Ahmadinejad is widely believed to be pursuing nuclear weapons that would give him the ability to carry out his apocalyptic religious views.

JOEL ROSENBERG, *NATIONAL REVIEW*

(AUGUST 10, 2006)

PREFACE

This book is about Iranian president Mahmoud Ahmadinejad. However, there are a few things this book *is not*.

First, it's not a biography. Certainly a book like this must contain some biographical and background information. But several excellent books are already available that present detailed facts and analyses about this man's life and political career.

Second, this book is not political in purpose. I did major in political science in college, and I have a law degree, but I'm certainly no expert in international politics. It will become obvious in this book that I believe Iran is the greatest threat to world peace today. But for the most part I will leave it to those more qualified than myself to discern the proper path to take with Iran and its current regime. I pray often for our national and international leaders, that God will give them wisdom in dealing with rogue nations like Iran. I believe that's the most effective thing I can do.

Third, this is not a book against Islam or Muslims. Many moderate Muslims don't condone Ahmadinejad's radical rhetoric. Even many in Iran strongly disagree with the direction he's taking their country. And his particular view of the end times is not shared by most Muslims, who are Sunni.

So, now that you know what this book is not, what is it?

This is a book about the end times. The apocalypse—both the Shiite Islamic version and the biblical scenario. While I'm no expert in history, politics, or Islam in general, I have spent a great deal of time studying what the Bible says about the future. And I've studied the Shiite Islamic view of the end times. The key to understanding Mahmoud Ahmadinejad is to understand *his* apocalypse and what it means for the future of the region, the world... and you.

The questions we face today are very real. And very alarming.

- Who is Mahmoud Ahmadinejad?
- What does he believe about the end of days?
- How does his view of the apocalypse shape his decisions?
- Who is the Islamic Mahdi or messiah?
- What's behind Iran's involvement in Iraq?
- Why does Ahmadinejad want to wipe Israel off the map?
- How do nuclear weapons fit into his plans for ushering in the apocalypse?
- Will Israel or the United States preemptively strike Iran's nuclear sites?
- Can diplomacy work?
- Could events we see in Iran be setting the stage for the end times?
- Does the Bible give any hope for the future?

We will explore these questions and many others in the pages that follow. As often as possible, I will try to allow Ahmadinejad to speak for himself. The book contains dozens of direct quotes because I believe it's important for you to hear him in his own words. His own disturbing words.

One thing is certain—Iran's president is committed to fulfilling his view of the apocalypse, and to do so he must obtain nuclear weapons, if he doesn't already have them, and destroy Israel and the West. As the nuclear showdown intensifies, the nations of the world will face monumental decisions.

The man at the center of it all is Mahmoud Ahmadinejad. The issue at the heart of Ahmadinejad is his apocalypse. It drives him. Compels him. Fuels him. And guides him. Far too many today are missing the integral linkage between his Shiite eschatology (his view of the end times) and Iranian foreign policy. If we fail to understand his apocalypse, we will never understand the current crisis—a crisis that could be paving the way for an epic struggle of literally biblical proportions.

One

THE WORLD'S MOST DANGEROUS MAN

We don't shy away from declaring that Islam
is ready to rule the world. We must prepare
ourselves to rule the world.

MAHMOUD AHMADINEJAD

The powerful army of the Islamic Republic of
Iran is in the service of peace and security and
is no threat to anyone. But in the face of enemies,
it is like a meteorite. It will cut off the hand of
any aggressor and leave the enemy covered in
shame.

MAHMOUD AHMADINEJAD

I have traveled to all the continents except for
one, and I know what is going on out there.
Everybody is eager to hear the Iranian people's
message.... The world is rapidly becoming
"Ahmadinejadized."

MAHMOUD AHMADINEJAD

Depending on your own beliefs, Ahmadinejad is either mystical or deranged. In either case, he is exceedingly dangerous.

CHARLES KRAUTHAMMER

The real danger is that Iran could become one gigantic suicide bomber.

BENJAMIN NETANYAHU

We have a strategy drawn up for the destruction of the Anglo-Saxon civilization....We must make use of everything we have at hand to strike at this front by means of our suicide operations or by means of our missiles. There are twenty-nine sensitive sites in the U.S. and the West. We have already spied on these sites and we know how we are going to attack them.

HASSAN ABBASSI (CHIEF STRATEGY ADVISER TO AHMADINEJAD)

A WORLD ON EDGE

As U.S. naval forces are conducting training exercises in the Persian Gulf, Iranian Revolutionary Guards fire on a U.S. ship, claiming it entered Iranian waters. Rumors of the confrontation spread like wildfire. Oil prices immediately spike. The United States quickly denies the report. In spite of this denial, rumors about the military confrontation in the Gulf spur panic buying in after-hours trading on March 27, 2007. The price of oil shoots up $5 to $68 a barrel in a matter of minutes. This is only the beginning. Speculators prepare for $150-a-barrel oil.

Then suddenly, prices fall back to $63 a barrel within a couple of hours.

It turned out to only be a rumor. Or was it?

Saudi Arabia has said that if the United States or Israel ends up in open confrontation with Iran, oil prices will triple overnight. That means oil at $150–$200 a barrel. That means $5, $6, or even $7 a gallon at the pump. The economic consequences will be catastrophic

But high gas prices will be only the first in a series of danger-ous dominos to fall if a misstep in the Gulf escalates out of con-trol. Terror alerts will go to level red in the homeland. Iran will unleash Hezbollah on Israel from the north and Hamas from the west; Syria might even join in. Tehran will stir an onslaught of sec-tarian violence in Iraq and turn it into a brutal bloodbath. Ameri-can troops will be caught in the crossfire and sustain heavy losses. The conflict will spiral out of control. Russia may feel the need to get involved. China could act to protect its vital oil lifeline in Iran. A chain reaction of triphammer blows will be set in motion.

The end result will be so catastrophic that no one probably has a complete picture of the destruction and confusion.

At this moment, this scenario is still fiction, but in truth it might not be in the near future. Iran is a powder keg waiting to explode. Iran is repeatedly, brazenly defying UN Security Council sanctions against its nuclear program. Threatening Israel with genocide. Stoking sectarian violence in Iraq. Capturing British sailors. Humiliating them in front of the world. Taunting the United States—"the Great Satan."

What's this all about? Is it just political jockeying? Is it a new muscular sense of Iranian nationalism reacting against Western "imperialism"? Or is there something more sinister behind it all?

Certainly many complicated, intertwined variables are involved in any political, international state of affairs. But no doubt remains that in Iran today an irrepressible force is at work—a relentless force with which there can be no successful negotiation or appeasement. A rabid ideology that seeks worldwide chaos, bloodshed, and war, all toward achieving its twisted, utopian fantasies.

And behind the ideology is a man. A man whose face is dominating the headlines. A man whose incendiary, bombastic bile is shocking the world. A man named Mahmoud Ahmadinejad. A man whose apocalypse may rock the world.

MAN WITH A MISSION

He stands a diminutive five feet four inches, smiles incessantly, blinks frequently, stares through squinting slitlike eyes, dresses plainly, and almost always wears his trademark tan jacket, which has become known as the "Ahmadinejad jacket."

Yet behind the dapper appearance and smiling persona lies the heart of a genocidal terrorist. Mahmoud Ahmadinejad, the president of Iran, is the most dangerous man on earth.

He makes Saddam Hussein look like Santa Claus. He is a son of the Islamic Revolution and played a major role in the takeover of the U.S. Embassy in Tehran and the ensuing 444-day Iran hostage crisis. He's a former member of the Iranian Revolutionary Guards. His organization participated in the bombing of U.S. marines in Lebanon. He and his organization were also involved in the horror of Pan Am Flight 103, which exploded over Lockerbie, Scotland on December 21, 1988. And he is now in command of a world-class army and air force and is actively seeking the ability to make and deliver a nuclear weapon. His goal is to bring about a "second revolution" in Iran.

THE OPENING SHOT

First impressions are important. Think about this for a moment: Ahmadinejad's very first public statement as president-elect on June 30, 2005, was to declare that the Iranian government was going back to its brutal beginnings. "Thanks be to the blood of the martyrs, a new Islamic Revolution has arisen and the Islamic Revolution of 1384 [the current Iranian year] will, if God wills, cut off the roots of injustice in the world. The era of oppression, hegemonic regimes, tyranny, and injustice has reached its end.... The wave of the Islamic Revolution will soon reach the entire world."[1] This was the way he first introduced himself to the world. His international audition. No subtle, quiet easing into office. No polite "Hi, I'm Mahmoud." But rather, an announcement of a new Islamic revolution that will sweep the globe.

The world has begun to awaken to Ahmadinejad and the threat he poses. Bridget Johnson minces no words when she calls him "arguably the world's most dangerous man."[2] Glenn Beck, almost every night on his CNN program, warns of the peril Ahmadinejad presents to the world. His face and his name—which is admittedly a tongue twister—is dominating world headlines.

THE WORLD TAKES NOTE

The *Newsweek* cover on February 19, 2007, featured closeup photographs of Ahmadinejad and U.S. president George W. Bush side by side, almost cheek to cheek, with the headline "The Hidden War with Iran: Skirmishes, Threats, Missed Signals. Why the Standoff Could Soon Turn Deadly." The cover article inside was titled "Rumors of Wars"—a clear reference to the prophecy of Jesus in Matthew 24:6.

Time's September 25, 2006, cover featured a large picture of Ahmadinejad and the headline "What War with Iran Would Look Like (And How to Avoid It)." Inside the magazine, *Time* recorded an interview with Ahmadinejad titled "A Date with a Dangerous Mind."

A photograph of Ahmadinejad with a prayer scarf draped over his shoulders filled *Newsweek's* February 13, 2006, cover, accompanied by the headline "How Dangerous Is Iran?" Two other headlines on the cover read "The Next Nuclear Threat" and "Radical Islam in Power." Inside, the main article on Ahmadinejad is titled "Devoted and Defiant," picturing Ahmadinejad reverently kneeling at the grave of Iran's revolutionary leader Ayatollah Ruhollah Khomeini.

U.S. News & World Report, on July 31, 2006, ran a cover story titled "Dangerous Liaisons: How Radicals in Iran Are Roiling the Middle East from Lebanon to Iraq." It included an article titled "An Impulse for Intrigue: Iran Has Really Big Plans, and Lots of Folks Have Really Big Headaches."

On November 13, 2006, *U.S. News & World Report* contained an article titled "The Dark Cloud on the Horizon: Why Israelis Eye a Potentially Nuclear-Armed Iran and Worry That a Cataclysm Can't Be Averted."

The cover story of the *Economist* in February 2007 sported a picture of a stealth bomber and the intriguing question "Next Stop Iran?"

The *Middle East* magazine, in its February 2007 issue, displayed the title "The Year Ahead." The only picture on the cover was a photograph of Mahmoud Ahmadinejad in the top left corner.

The cover of the *New Republic* (April 23, 2007) carried the caption "The Persian Paradox: What to Do About Iran" accompanied by a purposely distorted picture of Ahmadinejad.

All the world is taking note of this man. But what makes him so hazardous?

THE TRIPLE A OF AHMADINEJAD'S APOCALYPSE

Most informed people know by now that Mahmoud Ahmadinejad is an international troublemaker in charge of a rogue regime.

That he's a menace to world peace and Middle Eastern stability. But few people understand what drives him.

A prophetic dream drives him, a purported revelation from Allah. I call it *Ahmadinejad's apocalypse.*

I believe that the apocalypse of Ahmadinejad brings together the combustible mixture of three explosive ingredients:

1. Fanatical messianic ideology.
2. Vicious hatred of Israel and the West.
3. Hot pursuit of nuclear weapons.

These three key factors converge to make Ahmadinejad the world's most dangerous man. I like to call them the Triple A (AAA) of Ahmadinejad's apocalypse. Together, they form the signature of his regime. I'll briefly summarize them here, then expand on them in the next three chapters.

1. *Apocalyptic Ideology*

Ahmadinejad holds to a radical Shiite ideology—an ideological fervor run amok.[3] This fanatical worldview gives him a reckless, arrogant sense of invincibility inspired by his belief in the imminent return of the Mahdi—an Islamic messiah figure. Ahmadinejad dreams of a Shiite theocracy that will rule the Muslim world and ultimately the entire globe. He believes that the Mahdi will return in his lifetime—probably in the next two to three years.

Never before in modern history has a world leader so overtly flaunted his religious ideology and its influence on his policies. Yossi Melman and Meir Javedanfar observe: "Never before had an Iranian leader so publicly acknowledged his messianic belief. With

Ahmadinejad's election, this formerly taboo subject has become part of the central ideology of one of the most influential leaders of the world, with frightening implications."[4]

2. Anti-Semitism and Anti-Westernism

A second central component of Ahmadinejad's apocalypse is his vicious anti-Semitism and fierce hatred of the West. He has repeatedly threatened to wipe Israel, the "little Satan," off the map (and he calls the United States the "Great Satan"). For him, the United States and Israel are two main roadblocks that must be removed from the path of the Mahdi. Ironically, this is the same man who calls President Bush "Mr. Danger."[5] Is he really serious? Or is this just all talk?

People often wonder if or when Iran will attack Israel. The truth: they already have. Ahmadinejad took the first hostile step when he unleashed his terrorist, attack-dog proxy on Israel. The Hezbollah attack in July 2006 was phase one of Iran's war with Israel. Hezbollah—a Shiite terrorist group—is, in essence, an Iranian threat on Israel's northern border. Omar Fadhil notes, "It's common wisdom to say that the war between Hezbollah and Israel is a regional struggle that also includes Iran and Syria, who have supported and supplied Hezbollah. What seems to be less understood is that this is the first war between the Islamic Republic of Iran and Israel, via Iran's proxy Hezbollah, and that its overarching purpose is to advance Iran's ambitions to export the Islamic Revolution throughout the Middle East."[6]

The Hezbollah attack on Israel was the initiation of Ahmadinejad's apocalypse. It was a test run for Iran to try out its own command-and-supply capabilities, to probe Israel's defenses, and to gauge the reaction of the international community.[7]

The hostilities are far from over. Iran is arming Hezbollah for round two.

- Iran has provided Hezbollah with about twelve thousand rockets with a range of 26 to 120 miles—far enough to reach Tel Aviv.
- Iran has trained about 3,000 Hezbollah terrorists.
- Iran has set up at least 20 permanent missile bases in Lebanon.
- Iran has equipped Hezbollah with trucks to serve as launching pads for rockets.
- Iran has supplied experts in Lebanon to assist in targeting.[8]

Hezbollah's leader, Sheik Hassan Nasrallah, has pledged allegiance to Iran's supreme leader.[9] Former Deputy Secretary of State Richard Armitage calls Hezbollah the "A-team" of terrorist organizations. Hezbollah has metastasized throughout Lebanese culture and society, permeating every thread of the nation's fabric.[10] Ahmadinejad wants to turn Lebanon and Syria into armed Shiite outposts.[11]

Iran is also doing all it can to challenge the West. Ahmadinejad views the West, especially the United States and Britain, with disdain. He despises Britain because of its colonial policies of the past and the 1917 Balfour Declaration, which paved the way for the establishment of a Jewish homeland. The United States draws his ire because of its presence in the Middle East and its support of

Israel. He employs various names for the Western nations: "Global Arrogance," "Oppressor World," and "Infidel Front." He's made it no secret what he thinks of the West and that he would love nothing more than to destroy it.

Ahmadinejad initiates overt hostilities against the West politically, militarily, and economically. Politically, he defies the West and curries favor with Russia and China, who cover his back in the UN Security Council. Through his strong alliances with Hezbollah and Syria and attempts to subtly intimidate other Gulf States into turning against the United States, he's doing all he can to position Iran as the regional superpower.

Militarily, he has announced that Iran has developed a strategic "war preparation plan" for what he calls "the destruction of Anglo-Saxon civilization."[12] And he has already embarked on his plan as opportunities have arisen. He has actively manipulated the war in Iraq, maintaining a steady stream of Iranian troops and arms into Iraq to combat U.S. troops. And most recently in the news, he displayed bold aggression by kidnapping fifteen British sailors in a show of power.

On March 23, 2007, Iranian Revolutionary Guards seized fifteen British sailors who were patrolling for smugglers in the Persian Gulf. This sparked a thirteen-day standoff between London and Tehran. As the crisis unfolded, Ahmadinejad did all he could to stoke the fire. He said, "The British occupier forces did trespass our waters. Our border guards detained them with skill and bravery. But arrogant powers, because of their arrogant and selfish spirit, are claiming otherwise.... Instead of apologizing over trespassing by

British forces the world arrogant powers issue statements and deliver speeches."[13]

Finally, at an April 4, 2007, news conference, he presented a medal to the commander of the Iranian Coast Guard who captured the Brits. Then he droned on for about an hour about British and U.S. treachery, before springing his great proclamation: "On the occasion of the birthday of the great prophet [Muhammad] and for the occasion of the passing of Christ, I say the Islamic Republic government and the Iranian people—with all powers and legal right to put the soldiers on trial—forgave those 15.... The pardon is a gift to the British people."[14]

The scene of Ahmadinejad making each British sailor stand before him and thank him for his pardon was an open display of his pride and disdain. The look on his face during this spectacle showed the twisted pleasure he received from this act of humiliation. Ahmadinejad could easily exploit or even provoke another "trespass" into Iranian waters as justification for triggering a regional firestorm.

Economically, Ahmadinejad has traveled extensively and worked hard at maintaining old alliances and gaining new ones. He's trying especially to make friends with nations geographically close to the United States. He has developed a fast friendship with Venezuelan president Hugo Chavez, forged from their mutual disdain for the United States. Both Ahmadinejad and Chavez are ex-military populists.[15] Chavez is quickly turning Venezuela, the fourth largest source of U.S. oil imports, into a second Cuba—an enemy outpost within easy striking distance of the U.S. homeland.

Ahmadinejad and Chavez envision themselves as the final great hope against U.S. "imperialism." Together they agreed to create a $2 billion "strategic fund" to "help implement new projects in other world countries." Chavez noted, "Iran and Venezuela have clear and transparent objectives and strategies and will continue their resistance against imperialism."[16] Ahmadinejad views Chavez, with his country's oil reserves, as a convenient ally in his economic war with the United States. Part of his overall strategy is to use every chance he gets to hit the United States in the pocketbook.

3. *A*tomic *Weapons*

To support and accelerate the first two prongs of his strategy, Ahmadinejad has been relentlessly pursuing atomic weapons to destroy Israel and the West and so to inaugurate the advent of the Mahdi. Nuclear weapons are his powder-keg fuse, a key means to accomplishing his destructive mission. His bellicose stance on nuclear weapons is unyielding. Even as the United Nations places more sanctions on his nuclear program, he boasts that Iran will build more reactors and install more centrifuges for enriching uranium. Ahmadinejad has repeatedly said that Iran will never suspend its nuclear program, "even for one hour," and has promised that there will be no retreat, "even one millimeter back."

These three A's of Ahmadinejad's apocalypse are intricately intertwined, each dependent upon the other. Ahmadinejad's conviction concerning the imminent return of the Mahdi (first *A*) furnishes him with unwavering confidence, which allows him to act recklessly upon his hatred of Israel and the West (second *A*), most dangerously manifested in his desire to obtain nuclear weapons (third *A*).

Do you begin to see the world-shaking ramifications of his end-of-days messianism?

Is Peace Possible with This Man?

How can anyone hope for peace with someone who holds to this belief system? How can one possibly reason with an ideological zealot who resorts to so much bravado and grandstanding. A religious fanatic who may control nuclear weapons very soon. No amount of carrots or sticks would seem to work. This mentality was expressed well in 1992 by Hezbollah's former leader, Hussein Massawi: "We are not fighting so that you will give us something. We are fighting to eliminate you."

Of course, not all in Iran hold to this idea, but as we've seen, the majority of the leaders do, as does their Hezbollah attack dog. They subscribe to a violent, confrontational mentality that leaves no apparent room whatsoever for negotiated peace.[17] It's all or nothing for Iran and Ahmadinejad. And this attitude is fueled in large part by his apocalyptic vision of the future. A future that he believes is now. A future that he believes he can bring to pass.

Even King Abdullah II of Jordan has expressed grave concern over Ahmadinejad's grandiose vision. King Abdullah warned of the growing threat of what he calls a "Shiite Crescent" stretching from Iran, through Iraq, and all the way to southern Lebanon. The purpose of this crescent is to drive the United States from the Middle

East, destroy Israel, and challenge the Middle East nations whose Muslim populations are largely Sunni.[18]

Middle East expert and best-selling author Joel Rosenberg points out the integral linkage between Ahmadinejad's Shiite eschatology and Iranian foreign policy:

> Too many Western analysts are missing the central impor-
> tance of Shiite eschatology in Iranian foreign policy. They
> mistakenly believe that Iran's current leadership can be
> somehow cajoled into making peace with the West. Noth-
> ing could be further from the truth.
>
>   Mahmoud Ahmadinejad and his cadre of loyal mul-
> lahs are not being driven by the same goals and aspira-
> tions as are the diplomats in Washington, Brussels or at
> the United Nations. The President of Iran and his team
> fervently believe the Islamic Messiah is coming back
> soon, possibly as soon as this Spring. They are convinced
> that their divine mission is to create the conditions for
> the Mahdi's return. As a result, they are committed to
> instigating more anti-American violence in Iraq, not less.
> They are determined to obtain nuclear weapons at all
> costs, not negotiate away their atomic research and devel-
> opment program. What's more, they are deeply commit-
> ted to building political and military alliances with
> anti-Western powers, not finding accommodation with
> the West.
>
>   Bottom line: the leaders of Iran are preparing for an

apocalyptic war with the U.S. and Israel. It's not a question of "if" but "when."[19]

This is ultimately what makes Ahmadinejad the most dangerous man in the world. He is shaping official government policies from his messianic beliefs.[20] In short, here are the items that top Ahmadinejad's apocalyptic to-do list. Any of these pieces has the potential to spark another Middle East conflict:

- Unleash Hezbollah on Israel, arm and fund Hamas.
- Further destabilize the region.
- Build a Shiite Crescent from Iran to Lebanon.
- Tighten the oil noose around America's neck by controlling Middle East oil and deepening ties with Venezuela.
- Demonize the Jews and plan for genocide.
- Foment further sectarian violence in Iraq (by training, arming, and funding terror) and thereby weaken and humiliate the United States.
- Posture Iran to be the regional superpower.
- Pursue nuclear weapons at all cost.

That's what this book is about. Ahmadinejad's twisted view of the end times and how he is scheming to bring it into existence as soon as possible. How he is working feverishly to get all the pieces in place to launch his version of Armageddon.

Does this mean we don't try to talk with leaders like Ahmadinejad or give diplomacy a chance? No! In our current international environment, talking—and a lot of it—is a necessary part of the process. However, we need to do so with our eyes wide open, recognizing the seriousness of the stakes and the implications of his belief system. Recognizing that ultimately we don't have anything he wants—except surrender. This means that Iran is on a head-on collision course with Israel in particular and the West in general.[21] Interestingly, this is exactly what the Bible predicts for the end times.

AHMADINEJAD AND AN ANCIENT PROPHECY

Since his inauguration as president of the Islamic Republic of Iran, Mahmoud Ahmadinejad has been forging closer ties with many of Iran's neighbors. Russian-Iranian ties have deepened with Russia's sale of a nuclear reactor and high-tech missiles. Under the rule of Vladimir Putin and his old KGB associates, Russia is seeking to restore its influence in the Middle East and revive its cold war arms deals, while the United States flounders in Iraq.[22] Russia, a member of the UN Security Council, has consistently obstructed any stiff sanctions against Iran for its nuclear defiance, thus strengthening ties with Iran as a key part of their strategy.

Ahmadinejad has been something of a globetrotter during his brief tenure in office. He has bragged that the world is quickly becoming "Ahmadinejadized." During the summer of 2006 he visited Turkmenistan and Tajikistan to improve Iranian relations with these neighbors.

Ahmadinejad has also strengthened ties with Sudan. He visited the capital city, Khartoum, in early March 2007 and gave a lecture titled "Iran and the World." Sudan, led by President Omar al-Bashir, is considered by the United States to be a state sponsor of terror. Omar al-Bashir visited Tehran in April 2006. During that visit, Ahmadinejad made this statement at a press conference: "The Iranian and Sudanese nations and governments have a joint enemy that is constantly creating obstacles in the way of their advancement, and hatching plots against them."[23]

Sudan is a hardcore, radical Islamic nation. Osama Bin Laden was granted asylum in Sudan in the 1990s. Sudan has refused to allow the international community to deploy troops in Darfur, where most believe genocide is occurring.

During Ahmadinejad's visit to Khartoum, the two nations signed seven memoranda of understanding (MOUs) related to economic and political issues. The two nations have already expanded their mutual defense cooperation through the exchange of experts and stated their willingness to stand together against colonialism. Sudan declared its support of Iran in its quest for nuclear weapons, and Iran pledged to work to increase the volume of trade between the two nations. Iran is already involved in helping Sudan with water and electricity projects and is willing to assist Sudan with expertise in oil exploration.

It's bad enough, of course, that these radical Islamic countries and Russia are forging ever stronger ties in their jihad against Judeo-Christian civilization. But what is particularly important about these Iranian alliances is that they were foretold over twenty-five hundred years ago by the Hebrew prophet Ezekiel. Ezekiel 38 tells us that Persia, which is modern Iran, will be allied with Russia and a group of other Middle Eastern countries in an effort to destroy Israel. Bible scholars refer to this as the War of Gog and Magog.

And the word of the LORD came to me saying, "Son of
man, set your face toward Gog of the land of Magog, the
prince of Rosh, Meshech and Tubal, and prophesy against
him and say, 'Thus says the Lord GOD, "Behold, I am
against you, O Gog, prince of Rosh, Meshech and Tubal.
I will turn you about and put hooks into your jaws, and I
will bring you out, and all your army, horses and horsemen,
all of them splendidly attired, a great company with buckler
and shield, all of them wielding swords; Persia, Ethiopia
and Put with them, all of them with shield and helmet;
Gomer with all its troops; Beth-togarmah from the remote
parts of the north with all its troops—many peoples with
you." ' " (Ezekiel 38:1–6)

The ancient names in Ezekiel's prophecy do not exist on any
modern map, but it's possible to discover where these ancient lands
were in Ezekiel's day and identify the modern counterparts. The
name *Gog,* which means "high" or "mountain," is a title for the
leader of this invasion. Rosh is the modern nation of Russia.[24]
Ancient Magog was the land of the Scythians, which today is the
area we know as Central Asia. Turkmenistan and Tajikistan are
part of modern Magog. The other participants listed in this invasion in Ezekiel 38:1–6 are Meshech, Tubal, Gomer, and Beth-
togarmah, which are all in the modern nation of Turkey. The final
members of the invading force are Put (Libya), Persia (Iran), and
Cush (Sudan). Interestingly, in Ezekiel 38:5, Persia (modern Iran)
and Cush (modern Sudan) are mentioned right next to one another

as allies in this end-time battle. Iran and Sudan were listed side by side over 2,500 years ago by Ezekiel. This is incredible.

Persia and Cush are coming together. God, who knows the end from the beginning, is the only One who can accurately tell the future because He alone knows all things and controls all things. The precise correspondence of the Ezekiel prophecy with the events we see today confirms once again the truth of the Bible. This end-time coalition could be forming right before our eyes. And all this is occurring at the same time that Israel is back in her land, in desperate need of the peace treaty brokered by the West that will set the stage for the battle of Gog and Magog.

In a bizarre twist, Ahmadinejad, who believes he can usher in the apocalypse, may be part of God's plan to set the stage for the true end-time scenario predicted in the Bible.

But which of these eschatologies is true? Whose view of the apocalypse is correct? Is the prophecy in Ezekiel true, or is Ahmadinejad's apocalypse? How can we know? Is there any sure word about the future?

We'll answer this question later. Right now, let's explore who Ahmadinejad is, what makes him tick, what he believes about the end times, and what he's doing to make sure it happens.

Two

SON OF THE REVOLUTION: WHO IS MAHMOUD AHMADINEJAD?

Born to a blacksmith, educated as a revolutionary, trained as a killer, and derided by rivals as a mystical fanatic, Iranian President Mahmoud Ahmadinejad is easily cast as the personification of everything there is to fear about a nuclear Iran. But he may be worse than that.

BABAK DEHGHANPISHEH AND CHRISTOPHER DICKEY, *NEWSWEEK*

We say that we will be victorious. One day somebody asked me whether I was in relation with somebody when I say that we will be victorious. I answered: "Yes, I am in relation with God." In foreign politics, one should not be frightened or fear these people. Satan inspires Mr. Bush.

MAHMOUD AHMADINEJAD

I am a child of the revolution…and if there is a
danger for this revolution and our nation then I am
ready for it.

MAHMOUD AHMADINEJAD

Iran's new president was selected by the ruling Council of Guardian as a leader they trusted to uphold and
protect the values of the Islamic revolution. A career
Revolutionary Guards officer closely allied with the
Basij militia and the Ansar-e Hezbollah thugs who
whipped opposition activists with bicycle chains, he
had a terrorist's pedigree second to none.

KENNETH R. TIMMERMAN

THE SILENT COUP

On June 24, 2005, Mahmoud Ahmadinejad was elected the ninth
president of Iran in a runoff election against his rival, Hashemi
Rafsanjani. But Ahmadinejad didn't just win—he swept the election, capturing more than 17 million out of 27.5 million votes.
What made this so surprising was that Ahmadinejad came from
relative political obscurity to go toe to toe with a political heavy-
weight. Just a few days before the election, Rafsanjani was believed
to be slightly ahead.

In what has been called the "silent coup," Ahmadinejad was

brought to power by Iran's ruling elite and the military and para-military groups. It is generally agreed that Ahmadinejad's electoral triumph was not completely clean. There is strong evidence of "blatant ballot rigging."[1] Significant electoral interference was orchestrated by Ayatollah Mohammed Ali Khamenei and his hard-line followers. Why? Because Ahmadinejad is their man. He is one of them. With his background, experience, and training, he is someone they can trust to keep the dreams of the Islamic Revolution alive. He is an ardent zealot committed to their messianic end-time ideology. Like them, he sees his life's purpose as paving the way for the soon-to-come Shiite messiah. With the United States mired in Iraq, the West dependent on Middle East oil, and Hezbollah perched at Israel's northern border, now is their time. Now is their window of opportunity, and Ahmadinejad is the anointed catalyst.

When he took office in August 2005, Ahmadinejad became the first nonclerical Iranian president in twenty-four years. The world had little or no idea who he was. But that has changed dramatically. Ahmadinejad has taken the world stage by storm. He has announced his intention to export the Islamic revolution to the world and bring the Twelfth Imam out of hiding, leading ultimately to global Islamic rule. He's made no secret of his grand plans for his nation. He hasn't disappointed the hard-liners who swept him into office.

But how did he get to this place of prominence and influence? What does the world need to know about him? Here's a brief overview of his story.

FROM "THREAD PAINTER" TO "MUHAMMAD'S RACE"

Mahmoud Ahmadinejad's story begins in a remote part of the Iranian salt desert in north-central Iran.[2] He was born on October 28, 1956, and was given the name Mahmoud, a variant of the prophet Muhammad's name. He was his father's fourth child.

His father's name was Ahmad Saborjhian. He owned a barbershop in the village of Aradan. Not long after Mahmoud was born, his father moved the family to a neighborhood in northeastern Tehran in search of better opportunities. Before he moved, he changed his name. The family name Saborjhian comes from the Farsi word *sabor,* which means "thread painter." It refers to one of the most humble occupations in the traditional Iranian carpet industry.

Alireza Jafarzadeh, who brought Iran's covert nuclear program to light in 2002, describes the significance of the name change. "Ahmad expanded upon his first name, which means 'virtuous' and is another name used for the Prophet, Muhammad. He added *nejad* (race) to form Ahmadinejad, 'virtuous race' or 'Muhammad's race.' Name changing was common among many people who moved from villages to the cities, and Ahmad's choice reflected his intensely religious outlook." The family was "fanatically religious."[3]

SON OF A "BLACKSMITH"

It is often noted that Mahmoud Ahmadinejad came from humble beginnings. That his father was a "blacksmith" or "ironmonger."

Ahmadinejad has used this to his advantage to expand his populist platform and "man of the people" image. However, the Farsi word *ahangar* is more correctly translated "ironworker."[4] Ahmadinejad's father earned enough money working in the metal trades to purchase a home that was later sold for seventy thousand U.S. dollars, which is "a virtual fortune in Iran."[5]

A very telling story has surfaced about Ahmadinejad's father. In a television interview before the June 2005 presidential election, Ahmadinejad said that his father died in 1993 in an accident. Apparently, he told the story to gain sympathy and further bolster his image as a populist who endured great trials to rise to the top. However, a year after his election, Ahmadinejad attended his father's funeral. Ahmad Ahmadinejad did not die in an accident in 1993 as his son claimed; he died of a heart attack in 2006. Mahmoud Ahmadinejad even visited his father frequently during his illness.[6] Why would Ahmadinejad tell such a self-serving lie on national television? No one knows for sure, but this is clearly a glimpse into how eerily at ease he is with using deception and deceit to achieve his own ends.

CHILD OF THE REVOLUTION

Ahmadinejad was an excellent student and earned admission to the University of Sciences and Technology in the civil engineering program in 1975. He went on to achieve his doctorate in 1987 in engineering and traffic transportation planning. During his first year at the university, Ahmadinejad became closely tied to the political religious student movement of Ayatollah Ruhollah Khomeini. By his senior year he was an ideological firebrand and was the unquestioned leader of the movement. Ahmadinejad and his Islamic radicals played a significant role in the revolution that occurred in 1979, bringing Ayatollah Khomeini and the mullahs to power. Following the revolution he joined the ultraconservative faction of the Office for Strengthening Unity between universities and theological seminaries.[7]

The next milestone in Ahmadinejad's rise to power was his planning and participation in the Iran hostage crisis. Six of the fifty-two former U.S. hostages have stated that Ahmadinejad was one of their captors.[8] In early 2007, I watched a *Hannity & Colmes* segment on Fox News featuring David Roeder, one of the hostages who endured the 444-day ordeal in 1979–80. Mr. Roeder stated unequivocally that Ahmadinejad was one of the ringleaders of the hostage crisis and was present at many of his interrogations. He said that he could never forget the man's eyes and his frequent blinking. Roeder related one particular story involving Ahmadi-nejad: On one occasion, when Roeder refused to cooperate with Ahmadinejad's line of questioning, Ahmadinejad said through the translator, "We know where you live. We know that you have a handicapped child. We know what time he gets picked up for school. We know where. If you don't answer our questions as we like, we are going to chop off his fingers and his toes and send them one by one to your wife in a box."[9] As Roeder notes, it's hard to forget someone who issues that kind of threat.

During the brutal Iran-Iraq War (1980–88), Ahmadinejad voluntarily rushed to the western front to be part of the action. He joined the special forces of the Iranian Revolutionary Guards Corps (IRGC) in 1986. When the elite Qods (Jerusalem) Force of the IRGC was formed, he was appointed one of the senior leaders. As part of this force, "he directed assassinations in the Middle East and Europe.... He was reported to have been involved in planning an attempt on the life of Salman Rushdie."[10]

FROM GOVERNOR TO PROFESSOR

During the 1980s and early '90s, Ahmadinejad served several governorships. Then in 1997, after being removed from his post as governor general of Ardebil, he returned to teach engineering at Elm-o Sanaat University. But even during his teaching tenure his passion for the revolution boiled over. Those who worked with Ahmadinejad at the university in the 1990s "recall that he presented himself with radical, militant Islamic zeal that many others of his generation had shed."[11] While at the university he helped form a local chapter of a group known as Ansar-e Hezbollah (Followers of the Party of God). Alireza Jafarzadeh describes the organization: "This group, known for their signature black dress, acted as the mullahs' shock troops, attacking student gatherings and demonstrations, storming student dormitories, and beating up students and other opponents of the regime with chains, clubs, truncheons, and knives."[12]

MR. MAYOR

In April 2003, Ahmadinejad got the opportunity he was waiting for—to take his fundamentalist views mainstream—when he was appointed mayor of Tehran. As mayor, he wasted no time imposing his ideology on the populace. He radically reversed many of the more moderate policies instituted by reformist mayors. The following are a few of his controversial new directives. Ahmadinejad:

- turned cultural centers into prayer halls during the holy month of Ramadan
- used the podium at the town hall to preach his ideology
- closed fast food restaurants
- required male city employees to have beards and wear long sleeves
- ordered the construction of four women-only parks
- instituted separate elevators for men and women in municipal offices

The repressive nature of Ahmadinejad's administration earned him the name "the Iranian Taliban."[13] However, when he began to pursue the presidency, his speeches became much more "outlandish and mystical."[14] This was the world's first glimpse of what would come when he assumed the presidency in August 2005.

TROUBLE AT HOME

Ahmadinejad came to power on a populist platform promising to put Iran's oil wealth "on the dinner table," eliminate poverty, and reduce unemployment. However, the Iranian economy is reeling. Hyperinflation is pushing the economy toward a crisis.[15] Many are complaining that he has focused too much on fiery anti-U.S. rhetoric and not enough on the economy.[16]

One year into his presidency, Ahmadinejad's approval rating was enviable—as high as 70 percent.[17] The feeling was that people admired him for standing up to the United States over the nuclear issue. However, as he's moved further into his tenure, the country's economic problems have taken their toll and fueled domestic unrest and political opposition. These economic problems are nothing new in Iran, but Ahmadinejad is being held accountable for his campaign promises. Here are a few of the main trouble spots:

- Iran imports 40 percent of its oil.
- The price of bread, meat, and basic commodities has risen 25 percent.
- The value of the Tehran stock market has dropped 26 percent.
- Iran spends $20 billion a year subsidizing energy.
- Real estate is in short supply. (Every year 800,000 new families are formed in Iran, but only 450,000 housing units are built.)
- Apartment prices in Tehran are skyrocketing (3,000 percent increase since 1990).

What is more, in local elections on December 19, 2006, Ahmadinejad suffered major setbacks; he and his allies won just 20 percent of the 113,000 contested seats. Student protests have increased. In the summer of 2006, 50 economists wrote him a letter decrying his policies. And in January 2007, 150 members of Parliament signed a letter blaming Ahmadinejad for the raging inflation, rising unemployment, and failure to develop a budget on time.[18]

In light of these serious problems and the resulting unrest, one is quite justified in wondering, will the new president survive? After all, we all know that ultimately, "It's the economy, stupid."

I believe there are two answers to this question. First, it appears that as long as Ahmadinejad has the support of Ayatollah Khamenei, he is fine. Khamenei is the real power in Iran. Ian Bremmer believes that Ahmadinejad is too valuable to the ruling mullahs and Khamenei to be silenced. He says,

> Iran's ruling conservatives know they need a winning politi-
> cal issue to rally domestic support for an otherwise unpop-
> ular government. That's where the nuclear program—and
> public defiance of international pressure to renounce it—
> comes in. The clerics know that Iran's economic decline will
> not be easy to reverse. They also know that Ahmadinejad
> attracts most of the blame. And they know that their presi-
> dent has become the public face of defiance to Western
> pressure and chief defender of the nuclear program, a pow-
> erful symbol of Iran's sovereignty and growing international
> clout.... That's why, whatever their reservations about his
> rhetorical excesses and his inability to reduce inflation and
> unemployment, the mullahs still consider Ahmadinejad too
> useful to silence.[19]

AHMADINEJAD TIME LINE

1956—Born October 28 in Garmsar, Iran.

1970s—Attended the University of Science and Technology.

1979—Had high-level involvement in the U.S. hostage crisis.

1979—Was one of the first to join the Iran Revolutionary Guards Corps Intelligence Unit.

1980s—Known as "Golpa," he conducted intense interrogations of political dissidents.

1980–88—Carried out special operations in Europe and the Middle East during the Iran-Iraq War.

1980s—Served four years as deputy governor and governor of the cities of Maku and Khoy in northwestern Iran.

1980s—Served two years as an adviser to the governor general of Kurdistan Province.

1989—After the Iran-Iraq War, he joined the faculty of the University of Science and Technology, teaching civil engineering.

1993—Was appointed a cultural affairs adviser for the government, which involved imposing the Islamic beliefs of the mullahs on society.

1993–97—Served as governor general of Ardebil Province.

1997—Awarded his PhD in transportation engineering and planning.

2003—Appointed mayor of Tehran in April.

2005—Elected president of Iran in June and inaugurated in August.

This is an interesting theory, and it may well be correct.

Second, even if Ahmadinejad doesn't survive politically, the same radical, fundamentalist ideology that took over in 1979 will continue its stranglehold on the nation. Ahmadinejad is simply the front man for the mullah regime. The mouthpiece. The attack dog. It's the underlying ideology that's key. Ahmadinejad is its most ardent supporter and is very useful for advancing the "authorized" view of the apocalypse, but ultimately the ideology is larger than any one person.

For this regime, the apocalypse is what everything else is about.

With this brief biographical background in mind, let's investigate what's really behind Ahmadinejad's vision.

Prepare to be shocked.

Three

APOCALYPSE NOW: AHMADINEJAD'S FRIGHTENING VISION OF YOUR FUTURE

Iran is a mortal threat, and one also has to take account of the apocalyptic mood of Ahmadinejad and his circle.... Ahmadinejad and his group clearly believe, and I don't doubt the sincerity of their belief, that we are now entering an apocalyptic age, which will result in the triumph of their messianic figure.

BERNARD LEWIS

Ahmadinejad's fervent belief in the mystical elements of Shiite Twelver Islam suggests that he believes in the imminent return of the Disappeared Twelfth Imam (the Mahdi). Based on an analysis of his statements, one hypothesis is that he believes his role demands contributing to the outbreak of chaos in the Middle East to usher in Armageddon and the Day of Judgment.

WHAT MAKES TEHRAN TICK, IRAN POLICY COMMITTEE

Soon after becoming president, Ahmadinejad met with the foreign minister of an Islamic nation, who suggested that Iran seemed to be heading toward a crisis. Ahmadinejad replied that the crisis would prepare the arrival of the Mahdi, which would take place in few years. He later made the timetable more specific, saying the Mahdi would reappear in 2007.

YOSSI MELMAN AND MEIR JAVEDANFAR,
THE NUCLEAR SPHINX OF TEHRAN

I see the signs that Iran may be starting to launch the mullahs' version of an Armageddon, exploiting the religious beliefs of devout Shiites in the region. While this may sound more the stuff of prophecies than international relations, it is important to understand.

OMAR FADHIL

Our revolution's main mission is to pave the way for the reappearance of the Twelfth Imam.

MAHMOUD AHMADINEJAD

THE UNSEEN HAND

Ahmadinejad delivered a speech at the United Nations in September 2005, only one month after he assumed the presidency. Most in attendance were expecting another run-of-the-mill UN snoozer.

But Ahmadinejad's speech shocked the world. He spoke in apoca-lyptic terms and ended the speech with a messianic appeal to God to "hasten the emergence of your last repository, the Promised One, that perfect and pure human being, the one that will fill this world with justice and peace."

Ahmadinejad viewed himself as the messenger of God and believed that God's hand transfixed the audience during his UN speech. Anton La Guardia gave this report:

> In a video distributed by an Iranian Web site in November,
> Mr. Ahmadinejad described how one of his colleagues had
> claimed to have seen a glow of light around him as he
> began his speech. "I felt it myself too," Mr. Ahmadinejad
> recounts. "I felt that all of a sudden the atmosphere changed
> there. And for twenty-seven to twenty-eight minutes all the
> leaders did not blink.... It's not an exaggeration, because I
> was looking."[1]

Daniel Pipes highlights Ahmadinejad's own account of the UN address and his otherworldly experience:

> One of our group told me that when I started to say "In
> the name of God the almighty and merciful," he saw a
> light around me, and I was placed inside this aura. I felt
> it myself. I felt the atmosphere suddenly change, and for
> those twenty-seven or twenty-eight minutes, the leaders of
> the world did not blink.... And they were rapt. It seemed

as if an unseen hand was holding them there and had opened their eyes to receive the message from the Islamic republic.[2]

Talk about eerie and mystical. Ahmadinejad is a believer. His goal is clear: global domination. A mighty Islamic superpower that will be realized by the advent of the Islamic messiah, the Mahdi (the word *al-Mahdi* means "rightly guided one").

Ahmadinejad is firmly in the grasp of Mahdi mania. But Ahmadinejad doesn't want to sit around idly and wait for the Mahdi—he wants to speed up his coming. To advance the divine time table. Ahmadinejad has made his goal for the new regime dreadfully clear. His apocalyptic aspiration is to "establish an advanced, powerful, and exemplary society, so that it becomes a blueprint for the people of the world and thus ultimately serves as a platform for the reappearance of the Mahdi."[3] In a statement on November 15, 2005, Ahmadinejad explained:

> The people, in the last elections, proved their faith in the revolution and wish to see a revival of the Islamic revolution's ideals.... This revolution was in fact a continuation of the prophets' movement and, therefore, all political, economic, and cultural goals of the country need to be directed at materializing the Islamic ideals.... Followers of this divine school of Islamic thought are doing their best to pave the way for the urgent reappearance [of the Hidden Imam].[4]

Iran's new president wants to prepare the world for the Mahdi's coming and won't hesitate to pull the trigger to bring his view of the apocalypse to fruition.

Ahmadinejad's mystical preoccupation with the Mahdi lies at the very core of who he is and what he does. It fuels him. It defines his presidency. He is supremely motivated by his end-of-days messianism. Yossi Melman and Meir Javedanfar have summarized Ahmadinejad's passion very succinctly: "But of all his convictions, he believes in the arrival of the Mahdi most fervently.... Ahmadinejad will do what he can to make sure that happens, even if it means creating a crisis."[5] In order to understand him, his apocalypse, and what makes him so hazardous to the world, we must understand his intense fascination with the Mahdi.

SUNNIS AND SHIITES

Before examining Ahmadinejad's specific Shiite view of the end times, let's examine a little background on Islam (which means "submission") and the two major sects or branches under the Muslim umbrella—Sunni and Shiite. Presently, Sunnis represent about 85 percent of the world's 1.3 billion Muslims, and Shiites about 15 percent. Shiites, however, are the majority in Iran, Iraq, and Bahrain.

Islam began with the prophet Muhammad in the early seventh century in what today is Saudi Arabia. Muhammad wrote the Islamic holy book known as the Koran (which means "recitation" in Arabic). The Koran allegedly contains the revelation of the angel Gabriel to the prophet Muhammad. Islam enjoyed robust growth and success and remained unified during Muhammad's life.

The rupture of Islam into the two main sects occurred over 1,300 years ago. It was triggered by Muhammad's death in AD 632 and centers on the debate over who has the right to rule and interpret their scripture.[6] Shiites maintain that only descendants of Muhammad can be infallible and can rule, while Sunnis permit rulers from a broader group, as long as there is agreement among religious scholars.[7] The formal split occurred in AD 661. The feud between the two groups came to a head when the two sides met on a battlefield near modern Karbala on October 10, 680. Hussein, the son of Ali, who was a descendant of Muhammad, was the choice of the Shiites to lead the Islamic faithful. During the battle he was killed and decapitated. But rather than crushing the Shiite movement, the death of Hussein provided a martyr for it. The annual mourning over the death of Hussein is known to Shiites as Ashura, which is their most important ceremony. During the celebration of Ashura, the faithful march in the streets, beat their chests, wail in sorrow, and even flagellate themselves with swords and whips.[8]

This is a highly simplified introduction to the origin of Islam's two main branches, but it's enough to narrow our focus and gain an understanding of one strand of Shiite Islam, commonly known as Twelver Shiism or Twelvers. This is the view that drives Ahmadinejad and the mullah regime that runs Iran.

TWELVER THEOLOGY

After the prophet Muhammad died in AD 632, in the Shiite branch of Islam he was followed by a succession of imams (leaders). In Shiite Islam, the title *imam* is reserved for "Muhammad's male descendants through Ali and Fatima."[9]

Shiite Islam later split into three main divisions. The controversy between the groups centered on the number of imams who succeeded Muhammad.

- The Zaydis (called Fivers) recognized five imams.
- The Ismailis (called Seveners) recognized seven.
- The Ithna Ashari (also known as the Twelvers) recognized twelve imams. This group is the most popular of the three among Shiites.[10]

Twelver Shiite Islam is the official religion of Iran. According to their belief, the twelfth imam, who was given the name Abu'l-Qasim Muhammad and also known as Muhammad al-Muntazar ("Muhammad the Awaited One"), was born in AD 868 (year 255 on the Islamic calendar) in the Iraqi city of Samarra.[11] His father, Imam Hasan al-Askari, was the eleventh Shiite imam. He died in 874. It appears that the leaders were unaware of the birth of Muhammad, so they approached the eleventh imam's brother, Ja'far, assuming that he would take the role of imam. Ja'far seemed prepared to assume this mantle and entered the house of the deceased eleventh imam to lead the funeral prayers. Suddenly a young boy stepped forward and said: "Uncle, stand back! For it is

more fitting for me to lead the prayers for my father than for you."
After the funeral concluded, Ja'far was asked about the boy's identity and said that he didn't know who the boy was. After the funeral,
the boy was never seen again, and Shiite tradition maintains that
from that year the boy went into occultation or hiding.[12]

The doctrine of occultation, or *Ghayba,* plays a central role in
the Mahdi theology. The Mahdi allegedly went into hiding in 874
as a child with no sons, which created a major dilemma for the line
of succession. This crisis was resolved by the doctrine of the Hidden Imam, which teaches that the twelfth imam didn't die but
rather "disappeared" and is in "occultation" (hiding or absence) for
an unspecified period of time.[13] Followers of the Twelfth Imam
teach that he went into hiding due to hostile enemies who threatened his life and remains in hiding from ongoing danger to his
life.[14] Twelvers believe that the Hidden Imam or Mahdi disappeared in a well that's located in a cave in Samarra, Iraq. The well
is known as *Bi'r al-Ghayba*—"Well of the Occultation."[15] A
mosque was constructed over the cave, and the cave was parti-
tioned off by a gate called the Gate of Occultation. Shiites regularly
gather in the rooms of the cave to pray for the Mahdi's return.[16]

The Mahdi's period of occultation or absence is divided into
two parts: the Lesser Occultation and the Greater Occultation. The
Lesser Occultation lasted from AD 874 to 941. During this time
the Mahdi communicated with the outside world through four
successive agents who delivered his messages to his followers. When
the fourth of these human agents died in AD 941, the Hidden

Imam ceased communication, and the period known as the Greater Occultation began. The Greater Occultation is "the period of time when there is no agent of the Hidden Imam today."[17] For Shiites, the Greater Occultation continues today. The Hidden Imam is waiting for the time that Allah has decreed for his reappearance.[18]

Therefore, the main thrust behind Twelver belief is that the Twelfth Imam did not die but has been concealed from the eyes of man. His life has been miraculously prolonged until the day when he will manifest himself by God's permission. Twelvers believe that the Twelfth Imam will appear "as the divinely guided Mahdi at the end of time to vindicate his followers, restore the faithful community, and usher in a perfect Islamic society of justice and truth."[19] Expectation of his imminent return plays a key role in the popular experience of Twelvers today. Mahdi fever is growing among Shiites, especially in hard-liners like Ahmadinejad, and is spreading out to other Gulf States from its center in Iran.

An institute was established in Iran in 2004 for the study and dissemination of

---

MEET THE MAHDI

Various Titles of the Hidden Imam

Twelfth Imam

The Lost Imam

Lord of Command

Lord of the Age
(owner of time)

The Rightly Guided One

He Who Will Arise

Authoritative Source

The Awaited Imam

Remnant of God

information about the Mahdi. The institute has a staff of 160, and according to reports from inside Iran, it has considerable influence in the schools and children's magazines.[20]

APOSTLE OF THE APOCALYPSE

Mahdi mania is sweeping many areas in the Shiite Crescent. Iran, in particular, is simply mad about the Mahdi. Ahmadinejad is a driving force behind the furor. And the messianic fervor seems to be spreading. But Ahmadinejad's motivation runs even deeper. For him, the return of the Mahdi will do more than usher in an era of justice and peace. It will transform the entire world into one grand Islamic republic.[21]

When he was mayor of Tehran, Ahmadinejad wasted no time acting on his apocalyptic ideology. At great expense, he ordered the preparation of a detailed plan for the Mahdi's arrival in Tehran, including the designated route the Mahdi would take through the city.[22]

He also donated $17 million of government money to the Jamkaran Mosque in Iran, home of the Well of Request. Among Shiites, it's believed that the Jamkaran Mosque marks the exact spot where, for a brief moment, the Mahdi was miraculously "unocculted" or "unhidden." During this glorious, shining appearance, the Hidden Imam offered prayers to the Creator. Shiites flock to this site for its mystical power. Its symbolism is very similar to the shrine of Fatima in Portugal, where many Catholics believe the Virgin Mary appeared six times to three children in

1917.[23] According to Shiite tradition, if a person visits the mosque forty Tuesdays in a row with no interruption, he will see the Mahdi. In an article for the *Christian Science Monitor*, Scott Peterson describes the Iranian faithful fervently praying for the return of the Mahdi in the Jamkaran Mosque. "For those who believe, the devotion is real. Tears stream down the cheeks of two thousand men ripe for the return of the Mahdi, the Twelfth Imam they expect will soon emerge to bring justice and peace to a corrupt world. Eyes stare upward and arms open wide to receive God's promised salvation."[24]

It has been reported that all the members of Ahmadinejad's cabinet signed a written pledge of loyalty to the Mahdi. One of the cabinet members then brought the signed pledge to the Jamkaran Mosque and dropped it in the well to be received by the Mahdi.[25] After his election to the presidency, Ahmadinejad himself made an urgent visit to the Well of Request.[26] The purpose of the visit was to drop a piece of paper in the well bearing a prayer request, seeking an answer from the Mahdi. After this visit, he greatly increased funding for the mosque's renovations. Moreover, it has been reported that there are plans for the construction of a direct train line from Tehran to the Jamkaran Mosque.[27]

The first item on Ahmadinejad's agenda after he won the presidency was to pay a visit to the shine for the Ayatollah Khomeini—the father of the Islamic Revolution in Iran. The first meeting of his new cabinet was staged at the tomb of Imam Reza, the fourth Shiite Imam, and the only imam buried in Iran.[28]

Ahmadinejad is so focused on the Mahdi that the triumph of

his messianic figure appears everywhere. Even in his December 2006 "Christmas card" and New Year's wish to the world's Christians, Ahmadinejad again referred to the Mahdi, but also added in Jesus. The greeting said, "All I want to say is that the age of hardship, threat and spite will come to an end someday and, God willing, Jesus would return to the world along with the emergence of the descendant of the Islam's holy prophet, Imam Mahdi, and wipe away every tinge of oppression, pain and agony from the face of the world."[29] Of course, what he didn't say is that the Christians and Jews will have to die in order for this utopia to come into existence.

Ahmadinejad is a self-proclaimed apostle on a misguided mission from Allah. Anton La Guardia makes this unnerving observation about Ahmadinejad's "Apocalypse Now" theology:

All streams of Islam believe in a divine saviour, known as the Mahdi, who will appear at the End of Days. A common rumor—denied by the government but widely believed—is that Mr. Ahmadinejad and his cabinet have signed a "contract" pledging themselves to work for the return of the Mahdi and sent it to Jamkaran. Iran's dominant "Twelver" sect believes this will be Mohammed bin Hasan, regarded as the Twelfth Imam, or righteous descendant of the Prophet Mohammad. He is said to have gone into "occlusion" in the ninth century, at the age of five. His return will be preceded by cosmic chaos, war and bloodshed. After a cataclysmic confrontation with evil and darkness, the Mahdi will lead the world to an era of universal peace. This is similar to the Christian vision of the Apocalypse. Indeed, the Hidden Imam is expected to return in the company of Jesus. Mr. Ahmadinejad appears to believe that these events are close at hand and that ordinary mortals can influence the divine timetable. The prospect of such a man obtaining nuclear weapons is worrying. The unspoken question is this: is Mr. Ahmadinejad now tempting a clash with the West because he feels safe in the belief of the imminent return of the Hidden Imam? Worse, might he be trying to provoke chaos in the hope of hastening his reappearance?[30]

"KMADHI" (MAHDI RADIO)

In late 2006 and early 2007, official Iranian radio ran a lengthy series of broadcasts on the imminent appearance of the Mahdi, who will crush Islam's enemies and impose global Islamic Shiite rule. The purpose of this indoctrination was to prepare the people for the coming of the Hidden Imam and his miracles. The program, which was titled the *World Toward Illumination,* even speculated on specific dates that the Mahdi may be revealed.[31] There are even a new messiah hotline and Iranian news agencies devoted to the latest developments that portend the Mahdi's coming.[32]

Can you imagine this happening in the United States? This would be like having a series of government-sponsored radio programs on NPR discussing the book of Revelation and the signs of the coming of Christ.

The radio broadcasts outlined a fairly detailed Shiite eschatological scheme. The following is a distillation of the broadcasts' main points. Again, as you read, imagine this series being broadcast over official Iranian radio. Ahmadinejad's regime is preparing the people for his version of Armageddon. For a full text of the program, see appendix C.

OFFICIAL IRANIAN (SHIITE) ESCHATOLOGY

1. The Mahdi is coming soon.
2. Waiting for his coming is called "Awaiting Redemption."
3. The Imam Mahdi is a direct descendant of the prophet Muhammad.
4. He will appear suddenly.
5. A voice from the skies will announce his reappearance at the Holy Ka'ba in Mecca.
6. He will be joined by 313 of the most devoted, enlightened believers, who will pledge loyalty to him.
7. Only God knows the exact time of his appearance on earth, although some believe it will occur on a Friday or in conjunction with the spring equinox.
8. The Mahdi will remain in Mecca for a while after his reappearance.
9. He will then travel to Medina.
10. Sofyani, an archenemy, will attack Syria and Iraq and commit great crimes against humanity in Iraq.

11. The Mahdi will send troops who kill Sofyani in Jerusalem.

12. Jesus will return and serve as the Mahdi's lieutenant or deputy.

13. The Mahdi will establish the seat of his global government in the city of Kufa (in modern Iraq). His headquarters will be in the Sahla Mosque.

14. The earth will be filled with justice—a global government of peace and justice.

15. Islam will be the pinnacle of faith. All will convert to Islam. It will be the one pure, lasting world religion, practiced by all.

16. The world will experience astounding growth in science and technology as the Mahdi corrects all of man's scientific mistakes.

17. The earth will experience abundant rain, and vegetation will flourish—like an eternal springtime.

THE HOJJATIEH SOCIETY

In Arabic, the word *Hojjat*—"Authoritative Source"—is used as a title for the Mahdi.

Most experts believe that Ahmadinejad is a member of the clandestine, mystical Hojjatieh Society. This close ideological fraternity, which is the cult of the Mahdi, was founded in 1953 by Sheikh Mahmoud Halabi, a cleric from the holy city of Mashhad in northeastern Iran.[33] This school of thought was originally founded to combat the Baha'i faith, which teaches that Bahaullah, a nineteenth-century Persian nobleman from Tehran, was the Mahdi. For Hojjatieh, Bahaullah was an imposter, and the heresy of Baha'ism must be eradicated. Hojjatieh view themselves as the guardians and sentinels of the Mahdi.

Ed Blanche provides a concise description of Hojjatieh. He says it's a radical secret society that is "virulently anti-Western, anti-Sunni and committed to the arcane belief a true Islamic state can only be realized with the return of Shi'ism's hidden imam."[34] The core tenet of this group is a strong belief in the imminent reappearance of the Mahdi, who will usher in a worldwide Islamic empire characterized by peace, prosperity, and justice.

What's more, whereas most Shiites believe that God has appointed a time for the Mahdi's coming that cannot be affected by man, Hojjatieh devotees believe that they can encourage or hasten his arrival. They don't believe they can force the return of the Mahdi, but they do believe they can encourage his coming by stirring up chaos. This perilous Shiite precept is known as *taajil*.[35] For the sake of comparison, we could say that the Hojjatieh are Islam's version of a lunatic-fringe, end-time group like David Koresh and the Branch Davidians.

While numerous, often conflicting, accounts exist describing what will portend the Mahdi's return, the Hojjatieh believe that one of the significant signs is worldwide chaos, bloodshed, violence, and conflict. As Kenneth Timmerman observes, "As devotees of the Twelfth Imam, the Hojjatieh believe that only great tribulation will warrant his coming. Akin in some ways to V. I. Lenin's doctrine that worsening social conditions would hasten the advent of revolution, the Hojjatieh believe that only increased violence, conflict, and oppression will bring the Mahdi's return."[36] But Hojjatieh also recognize many lesser signs of the Mahdi's coming. After Ahmadinejad's appearance at the United Nations in September 2005, Ali Davani, an important figure in the powerful Ansar-e Hezbollah political organization and a close Ahmadinejad ally, publicly declared that Ahmadinejad's UN speech was "one of the signs indicating the appearance of the Mahdi."[37]

Thus it seems that the Hojjatieh believe in many signs of the Mahdi's coming, and hard-core Mahdists are seeing the signs everywhere. For them, the signs are all pointing in one direction— the Mahdi is coming. Very soon. And Ahmadinejad and his cadre of ardent ideologues are doing all they can to make it happen. Chaos, even purposefully caused by "the faithful," is a necessary condition for the Mahdi's reappearance.

Raymond Whitaker provides this insightful look into Ahmadinejad and his Hojjatieh roots:

> More worrying for some is that Ahmadinejad is closely identified with the cult of the "hidden imam," the twelfth and last of the line of imams revered by Shia Muslims. In a clear parallel with Jewish and Christian visions of Armageddon, Shias believe the imam zaman will return at a time of great turmoil to defeat the forces of evil; recently the president urged Iranians to work hard for this moment. As one

commentator pointed out, this was like Tony Blair telling Britons to prepare for the Second Coming. The most extreme zealots, a group called the Hojjatieh, say total chaos should be created to hasten the coming of the Mahdi… This explains his reckless attitude, say his critics. If the final triumph of Islam can be brought closer by provoking a nuclear war with Israel or America, why hold back?[38]

Soon after his inauguration in August 2005, Ahmadinejad declared that the real ruler of Iran was the Twelfth Imam and that government policy and decisions would be directed by the goal of hastening his coming.[39] Ahmadinejad promptly began appointing Hojjatieh faithful to his cabinet and throughout the Iranian bureaucracy. He surrounds himself with fellow Mahdists.[40] As a Hojjatieh member, or at least a sympathizer, Ahmadinejad believes that his role as president demands "contributing to the outbreak of chaos in the Middle East sufficient to usher in Armageddon and the Day of Judgment."[41]

PROFESSOR CROCODILE

One of the shadowy figures behind Ahmadinejad, and an important figure in Hojjatieh, is Ayatollah Muhammad Taqi Mesbah Yazdi. His nickname is Professor Crocodile. He's called Professor because he heads up two Shiite schools in Qom, Iran, and he's called the Crocodile because *Mesbah* rhymes with *Temsah,* which is Farsi for "crocodile."

Yazdi, an ultraorthodox radical, is recognized as Ahmadinejad's mentor, the shaper of his worldview, the hidden power behind the scene. He's known as the chief ideologue of Hojjatieh and will stop at nothing to realize the Hojjatieh dream. He has also been given the name "the Red Cardinal" for ordering the assassination of numerous Iranian dissidents in the late 1990s.[42] Yazdi has long advocated "martyrdom operations" to battle the "enemies of Islam."[43]

During the elections in June 2005, Yazdi issued a *fatwa* (religious decree) urging the faithful to consider it their religious duty to vote for Ahmadinejad.[44] Yazdi was a student of the Ayatollah Khomeini and now heads the Ayatollah Khomeini Institute in Qom. Posted in the lobby of the institute is a board displaying the number of days since the Mahdi went into hiding.[45] According to Kenneth Timmerman, Ahmadinejad, with Yazdi as his adviser, is "transforming these messianic beliefs into government policies."[46] Yazdi, like Ahmadinejad, nurses a vicious hatred for Jews.

To further his influence on Ahmadinejad, Yazdi has appointed one of his students, Mojtada Samare Hashemi, as Ahmadinejad's personal guide and mentor in messianic issues.[47] Ahmadinejad calls him Brother Samare. He's far more extreme in his messianism even than Ahmadinejad.[48]

SIGNS OF THE MAHDI'S RETURN

Fervent expectation of the Mahdi's return plays an important role in the Twelver tradition.[49] Muslims disagree among themselves about the signs that will herald the Mahdi's return, but here are a few very specific ones that usually end up near the top of most lists:

Five Keys Signs of the Mahdi's Manifestation[50]

1. The rise of a fighter from Yemen called Yamani, who attacks the enemies of Islam.
2. The rise of an anti-Mahdi, known as the Sofyani. He will appear along with another anti-Mahdi militant called Dajal. He is often compared to the Antichrist. Sofyani's uprising will occur in Mecca exactly six months before the Mahdi's reappearance.
3. The voice of the angel Gabriel will be heard from the sky, calling the faithful to rally around the Mahdi.
4. The destruction of Sofyani's army.
5. The death of a holy man named Muhammad bin Hassan, known as the "pure soul." The Mahdi will appear in Mecca fifteen days after he is killed.

While these are the five key *specific* signs of the Mahdi's return, there are other more general signs: "the inability to distinguish between men and women due to cross-dressing, a time of moral corruption, a degraded state in Islam, deadly plagues, and the death of 80 percent of the world's population in a massive war."[51] According to their view, the time of the end will be a general time of warfare and universal chaos. There are other prophecies that are viewed as referring to the radio and airplanes at the time of the Mahdi's reappearance.[52]

SHOW ME THE MAHDI

1. He won't come in an odd year (using the Islamic calendar).
2. He will make his appearance in Mecca.
3. He will travel from Mecca to Kufa (in Iraq).
4. He will be a young man of medium stature, with a handsome face; long, beautiful, black hair that flows onto his shoulders; and a shining face.
5. He will be forty years old at the time of his emergence.
6. He will remove all injustice, and the entire world will experience overflowing prosperity.
7. Jesus will return with him and be his deputy.
8. The 313 who fought with the prophet Muhammad at the battle of Badr will also return.
9. People will recognize him because there will be an angel above his head shouting, "This is the Mahdi; follow him."
10. The other imams and prophets of former ages will return.
11. He will wear a ring that belonged to King Solomon.
12. He will carry the wooden staff that Moses held when parting the Red Sea.
13. His army of 313 will grown into 50,000 (50 will be women).
14. He will rule for seven years.

THE IRAQ WAR AND THE MAHDI

Many people probably don't realize that the majority of Iraq's population follow the Shiite branch of Islam. Shiites number about seven million of Iraq's total population of twelve million, or about 55–60 percent. Saddam Hussein and his Baath Party were Sunnis. So during his reign the Sunni minority brutally suppressed the Shiite majority. That's one reason for much of the sectarian violence in Iraq today. For many Shiites, it's payback time. But there's even more to the ferocious fighting. Iran is working overtime to stoke the violence. Certainly Iran is doing this for political reasons. Iran fought a bloody, costly war against Saddam and the Sunni minority from 1980 to 1988. Also, Iran is seizing the opportunity to inflict damage on the United States, humiliate Britain, and further pummel a beleaguered George W. Bush. But there's also a religious element to Iran's involvement in Iraq that is often overlooked.

In Shiite eschatology, Iraq is closely linked to the Mahdi in several important ways. First, Iraq is the birthplace of the Mahdi. Second, his occultation or divine cloaking began in a cave near Samarra, Iraq. Third, after his reappearance he will establish his world capital in Kufa, Iraq, which is about one hundred miles south of Baghdad. The linkage of the Mahdi to this area is why the main Shiite stronghold in Iraq is in the south. Southern Iraq is a hotbed of Mahdist fanatics.

This became apparent, for example, on January 28, 2006, when American and Iraqi soldiers clashed with an apocalyptic group known as the Soldiers of Heaven. The six hundred to seven hundred cultists were led by Dhia Abdul Zahra, who claimed he was the messiah. The group planned to storm the holy city of Najaf (near Kufa) and assassinate some top Shiite clerics. Members of the cult believe that the killing of the hierarchy in Najaf is one of the signs of the Mahdi's return, so they were trying to make it happen. When they were initially approached by Iraqi police and ordered to disband, they replied, "I am the Mahdi and I want you to join me. Today will be the day of his coming."[53] During the battle with American and Iraqi troops, the cultists repeatedly tapped into their radio frequencies with a chilling message: "Imam Mahdi is coming."[54] According to experts, dozens of Shiite factions and death cults with similar end-time views have sprung up all across southern Iraq. They are deeply frustrated and angry that Shiite leadership is not doing anything to hasten the Mahdi's coming.

The largest player in southern Iraq is the "Mahdi Army," a militia group led by the fiery Shiite cleric Moqtada al-Sadr. Some of his followers believe he is the Mahdi himself. Iran is his chief ally and supporter. He mysteriously disappeared to Iran to gather further support from his fellow Mahdi fanatics. But he recently resurfaced again in Iraq.

Even in Baghdad, in the eastern part of the city, banners and writings on walls have suddenly proliferated, carrying religious messages that refer specifically to the Hidden Imam. It looks to many observers like the way is being paved for the imminent arrival of the imam to be announced through the *Mumahidoon* (those who pave the way for the imam)—the descriptor that al-Sadr and his followers apply to themselves.

Shiite extremists in Iraq view U.S. occupation as an attempt to prevent the Mahdi from reappearing there.[55] Ahmadinejad and his fellow Mahdists are tapping into the apocalyptic mania in Iraq and going to great lengths to foster it. They believe that expelling the United States from Iraq will set the stage for the Mahdi's return to the place of his birth and the ultimate establishment of his world capital in Kufa.[56]

KILLING THE JEWS WILL BRING THE MAHDI

The official Iranian news agency, Fars, which is close to the conservative circles in Iran, published a statement by Ayatollah Hossein Nouri-Hamedani, one of the leading religious voices for the Iranian regime. In his speech he states that fighting the Jews will pave the way for and hasten the appearance of the Hidden Imam. The Fars News Agency quickly removed the report from its Web site only a few hours after its publication, and other conservative Iranian media channels refused to cite the report.[57]

According to the Fars report, Ayatollah Nouri-Hamedani met with members of the Mahdaviyat Studies Institute. The institute focuses on the coming of the Hidden Imam. The ayatollah extolled the institute's work and insisted that the religious seminaries in Qom conduct more in-depth research in religious texts and *hadith* concerning the Hidden Imam. Discussing Shiite religious texts, Ayatollah Nouri-Hamedani said, "One should fight the Jews and vanquish them so that the conditions for the advent of the Hidden Imam will be met." He also said, "In the texts it is told that the Hidden Imam will remove the yoke of humiliation from mankind's neck. Therefore it is clear that prior to the advent of the Hidden Imam, Arrogance [a common epithet for Western powers, especially for the United States] and colonialism rule the world."[58]

It's clear from his statements that he believes that the world stage is ready for the appearance of the Mahdi. He sees Western "arrogance" and Zionism as two impediments that must be eliminated before the Mahdi will make his appearance.

This ideology fits hand in glove with the bombast that Ahmadinejad consistently spews out.

PUTTING THE PUZZLE TOGETHER

Let's pause now to put some of the pieces together. The strain of Shiite Islam that fuels Ahmadinejad holds to several core beliefs, which have potentially catastrophic consequences:

- The only hope for the world is the Mahdi's coming.
- Chaos and rampant violence in the region are among the key signs leading to the main battle in which the Imam will return to lead Shiites to victory. The Mahdi will come only when the world is suffering the death throes of war and chaos.

- Followers of the Mahdi can accelerate his coming. His reappearance must be prepared for by his followers in a particular sequence of events.
- The elimination of the Western "imperialists" and Israel will hasten the end.
- Ahmadinejad would not hesitate to trigger or provoke a regional or global war to set the stage for the end of the world.

Ahmadinejad is preparing the Iranian people and the world for his vision of the final great conflagration. He believes it will occur in his lifetime. He's fifty years old.

Let me repeat Joel Rosenberg's succinct and sobering summary, quoted earlier: "Bottom line: the leaders of Iran are preparing for an apocalyptic war with the U.S. and Israel. It's not a question of 'if' but 'when.'"[59] He continues:

Ahmadinejad made his Islamic eschatology even more clear. He told followers that he believed the end of the world was rapidly approaching, and that the way to hasten the coming of the Messiah was to launch a global jihad to annihilate Israel and the United States. He also told followers that the "Mahdi" is already on the planet, but has not yet chosen to reveal himself. What's more, Ahmadinejad has said that he has personally been in contact with the "Mahdi" and received instructions from him, instructions that are apparently leading Iran to prepare for an apocalyptic war to annihilate Judeo-Christian civilization as we know it.[60]

With this set of beliefs as his framework, what would be the quickest, surest way to plunge the world into a maelstrom of chaos, bloodshed, and war? What would be the most effective way to put out the welcome mat for the Mahdi? Ahmadinejad could leverage numerous doomsday scenarios, bring the world to the brink of annihilation, and precipitate the Mahdi's reappearance. He could continue to brazenly threaten Israel, humiliate and defy the West, and bait them into a preemptive strike against his nuclear network. He could then justify any degree of retaliation. Or he could stage a military "mishap" in the Persian Gulf, similar to the kidnapping of the fifteen British sailors, which could easily escalate into a regional war. Or he could increase Iranian participation in the war in Iraq and force America's hand. Or Ahmadinejad could pull the trigger himself by ordering an all-out Hamas-Hezbollah offensive against Israel or even a nuclear hit in the heart of Israel.

Ahmadinejad could employ any of these scenarios, or some other evil plan, but one central goal is the destruction of Israel. Wiping Israel off the map is the nonnegotiable.

Four

NEW HITLER—NEW HOLOCAUST

Iran today is in the grip of yet a new wave of extremists.
Its president, Mahmoud Ahmadinejad, is a revolutionary firebrand who has directly threatened the West. In
his own words, "We are in the process of an historical
war between the World of Arrogance [i.e., the West] and
the Islamic world." His foreign policy ambition is an
Islamic government for the whole world, under the leadership of the Mahdi, the absent imam of the Shiites—
code language for the export of radical Islam. And he
casts himself as Hitler reincarnated, calling for Israel to
be "wiped off the map." Who can think that Iran poses
no threat to world peace? History tells us that when
madmen call for genocide, they usually mean it.

MORTIMER ZUCKERMAN

In each generation there are those that rise up seeking
our destruction. But since Hitler, there has not risen such
a bitter enemy as Iran's president, Ahmadinejad, who
openly declares his desire to annihilate us and his development of nuclear weapons in order to carry out his desire.

BENJAMIN NETANYAHU, FORMER ISRAELI PRIME MINISTER

The use of even one nuclear bomb inside Israel will destroy everything.... It is not irrational to contemplate such an eventuality.

AKBAR HASHEMI RAFSANJANI, CHAIRMAN OF IRAN'S
EXPEDIENCY COUNCIL (2001)

Whether you like it or not, the Zionist regime is on the road to being eliminated.

MAHMOUD AHMADINEJAD

ANNOUNCING ANNIHILATION

Of all the bombastic, incendiary statements President Ahmadinejad has made—and there are many—probably the best known is his declaration that Israel must be wiped off the map. Of course, anti-Semitism is nothing new. The persecution and pogroms against the Jews stand as historical witnesses to centuries of mistreatment and attempted extermination. But Ahmadinejad is not just any anti-Semite. He is an avowed proponent of the destruction of the State of Israel. A new Hitler. And what makes him especially deadly is that this virulent, deadly determination is part of his overall view of the end times. For Ahmadinejad, the conquest of the Jews is part of the overall chain of events that must occur in order for the Mahdi to return. For him, anti-Semitism is not some personal flaw or ignorant bigotry. It's deeply ingrained in the fabric of his belief system. It's a fundamental principle of his ideology. His view of the apocalypse compels him to hate the Jews and call for their conquest.

Not only is Ahmadinejad's anti-Semitism foundational to his ideology—it is also very well orchestrated. His strategy is as simple as it is evil. He has implemented a straightforward, yet savage, three-pronged attack against the Jews.[1] These three prongs are intricately interrelated and state-directed:

1. *Direct attack:* Ahmadinejad employs the tactic of blunt force. A direct, frontal attack. He persistently preaches the destruction and elimination of Israel.

2. *Demonization:* Ahmadinejad constantly dehumanizes the Jews and the State of Israel, accusing them of war crimes and worse. These first two prongs are eerily similar to Hitler's buildup to genocide.

3. *Denial of the Holocaust:* It's difficult to demonize a group of people who are considered victims of terrible persecution and injustice. Therefore, the third prong of Ahmadinejad's anti-Zionist strategy is to vehemently deny the historicity of the Jewish Holocaust at the hands of Hitler and the Nazis, to eradicate any notion that the Jews are victims. He believes the Holocaust "myth" is holding the West hostage and is just a pretext for Israel's very existence. Ahmadinejad implies that the only justification for Israel's existence is the Holocaust; therefore, if he can successfully deconstruct that chapter of history, he can substantiate his call for Israel's elimination.

Let's look more closely at each of these three prongs of Ahmadinejad's plan to get rid of the Jewish people worldwide and the State of Israel. And let's look at the justifications for asserting that he has become a new Hitler threatening a new Holocaust.

DIRECT ATTACK—PAVING THE WAY FOR GENOCIDE

The first segment of Ahmadinejad's anti-Semitic strategy is to fiercely denounce and degrade the Jews publicly and call for their annihilation. But this is nothing new in Iran. In September 1998, Iran's Revolutionary Guard Corps, of which Ahmadinejad was a member, introduced its new Shahab-3 missile during a military parade in Tehran. During the parade a huge banner bore this shocking slogan in both Farsi and English: "Israel must be wiped off the map."[2]

Ahmadinejad did not bring anti-Semitism to the Iranian ruling regime; he has simply taken up the mantle of the Ayatollah Khomeini. Ahmadinejad is doing exactly what Hitler did in the 1930s. Like Hitler in *Mein Kampf,* Ahmadinejad is boldly announcing his intention to commit mass murder.[3] Here's a small sample of some of the shocking statements by Ahmadinejad about the Jews, the Holocaust, and the State of Israel…in his own words.[4]

June 3, 2007

The countdown to the disappearance of this regime was started by Hizbullah fighters, and with the help of all the Lebanese and Palestinian fighters we will witness the disappearance of this regime in the near future.[5]

April 18, 2007

Following a speech by Ahmadinejad in Tehran in honor of Army Day, the army paraded in front of the president and many of Iran's most senior military officials. The display showed off regiment after regiment of ground forces, tanks, a new set of drones and medium-range Nazeat (Meteor) missiles, one of which was inscribed "Death to Israel." Ahmadinejad said, "Our people hold out the hand of friendship to all the peoples. We want friendly and just relations with all the peoples except the Zionist regime."[6]

March 2, 2007

"There is no place in the world that suffers from divisions and wars unless America or the Zionists' fingerprints are seen there.... We have to pay attention to the devils [U.S. and Israel] who want to cause divisions among us" (during a speech in Khartoum, Sudan).

"The Zionist regime was created by the British, brought up by the Americans, and commits crimes in the region with their support. The Zionist regime is the symbol of hedonism and the incarnation of the soul of the oppressive powers" (during a speech in Khartoum, Sudan).

February 28, 2007

"Zionists are the true manifestation [incarnation] of Satan"[7] (during a speech in Khartoum, Sudan).

January 23, 2007
"The United States and the Zionist regime of Israel will soon come to an end of their lives."[8]

December 12, 2006
"Thanks to people's wishes and God's will, the trend for the existence of the Zionist regime is downwards and this is what God has promised and what all nations want.... Just as the Soviet Union was wiped out and today does not exist, so will the Zionist regime soon be wiped out" (comments to Iran Holocaust Conference).

November 13, 2006
"Israel is destined for destruction and will soon disappear."

Israel is "a contradiction to nature; we foresee its rapid disappearance and destruction."

October 20, 2006
"The West should pick up the Zionist regime by the arms and legs and remove it from the region....

"The life of this regime depended on military threat, military force, and the legend that it was invincible. Today, with God's grace, this false legend has collapsed, with the help of the young believers of Palestine, and thanks to the believing, self-sacrificing commanders of Hizbullah. Today, the Zionists do not feel secure even in their own homes, anywhere in the world....

"Today, this community, which was gathered by force, and under false pretexts, and whose members were joined to one another by a paper-clip, in order to create a false illusion of a nation.... Today, they have fallen apart. I declare here, loud and clear: with God's grace, this regime has lost the philosophy of its existence....

"This [Zionist] regime is on the verge of death."[9] (These quotes come from an address that aired on Jaam-e-Jam 1 television in Iran.)

August 6, 2006
"They [Israelis] kill women and children, young and old. And, behind closed doors, they make plans for the advancement of their evil goals" (quoted by Khorasan Provincial television).

August 2, 2006
"Are they human beings?... They [Zionists] are a group of blood-thirsty savages putting all other criminals to shame"(quoted by Iranian television).

July 27, 2006
"The occupying regime of Palestine has actually pushed the button of its own destruction by launching a new round of invasion and barbaric onslaught on Lebanon" (quoted by Islamic Republic News Agency via the Associated Press).

July 16, 2006
"The Zionists think that they are victims of Hitler, but they act like Hitler and behave worse than Genghis Khan" (quoted by the Iranian News Agency).

May 11, 2006

Israel is "a regime based on evil that cannot continue and one day will vanish" (to a student rally in Jakarta, Indonesia).

April 24, 2006

"We say that this fake regime [Israel] cannot logically continue to live. Open the doors [of Europe] and let the Jews go back to their own countries" (in a news conference).

April 14, 2006

"If there is serious doubt over the Holocaust, there is no doubt over the catastrophe and holocaust being faced by the Palestinians. Holocaust has been continuing in Palestine over the past sixty years" (in a speech at the opening of the "Support for the Palestinian Intifada" conference on April 14–16, hosted in Tehran).

February 23, 2006

"These heinous acts are committed by a group of Zionists and occupiers that have failed. They have failed in the face of Islam's logic and justice.... They invade the shrine and bomb there because they oppose God and justice.... But be sure, you will not be saved from the wrath and power of the justice-seeking nations by resorting to such acts" (in a speech broadcast on state television, in which Ahmadinejad suggested that the bombing of a major Shiite shrine in Iraq by Sunni insurgents was plotted by Israel and the United States to divide Muslims).

January 2, 2006

"[The creation of Israel after World War II] killed two birds with one stone [for Europe].... [The objectives achieved by Europe were] [s]weeping the Jews out of Europe and at the same time creating a European appendix with a Zionist and anti-Islamic nature in the heart of the Islamic world.... Zionism is a Western ideology and a colonialist idea...and right now it massacres Muslims with direct guidance and help from the United States and a part of Europe.... Zionism is basically a new [form of] fascism" (in written answers to questions from the public reproduced in several Iranian newspapers).

December 20, 2005

"Any power that is close to God will survive while the powers who are far from God will disappear like the pharaohs. Today, it is the United States, Britain and the Zionist regime which are doomed to disappear."

December 13, 2005

"If the killing of Jews in Europe is true and the Zionists are being supported because of this excuse, why should the Palestinian nation pay the price?" (comments published on Iranian state television's Web site).

October 28, 2005

"They [International Zionist and Expansionist Policies of the World Arrogance, i.e., the United States and Israel] are cheeky humans, and they think that the entire world should obey them. They destroy Palestinian families and expect nobody to object to them" (defending his earlier comments).

"Any nation that recognizes Israel's existence will "burn in the fire of the Islamic *umma* [nation]."

October 26, 2005

"Israel must be wiped off the map.... The establishment of a Zionist regime was a move by the world oppressor against the Islamic world.... The skirmishes in the occupied land are part of the war of destiny. The outcome of hundreds of years of war will be defined in Palestinian land" (in an address to four thousand students at a conference titled "The World Without Zionism").

Citing his mentor, Ayatollah Khomeini, Ahmadinejad stated, "The Imam said: 'This regime that is occupying Qods [Jerusalem] must be eliminated from the pages of history.'" Commenting further on this, Ahmadinejad said, "This sentence is very wise. The issue of Palestine is not an issue on which we can compromise.... Very soon this stain of disgrace [Israel] will be purged from the center of the Islamic world—and this is attainable."[10]

THE WORLD WITHOUT ZIONISM

On October 26, 2005, Iran sponsored an entire conference named "The World Without Zionism." The title of the conference leaves nothing to the imagination. Ahmadinejad wants Israel removed from its ancient homeland. At the conference, Ahmadinejad addressed over four thousand students, at one point issuing this alarming statement: "They say how could we have a world without America and Zionism? But you know well that this slogan and goal can be achieved and can definitely be realized." When he made this comment, he motioned at a podium that showed the name of the conference. These photos were widely published by media outlets from Al Jazeera to the Associated Press. However, what Ahmadinejad was actually motioning toward, and what most people never saw, was only evident in the wider shot. According to WorldNetDaily, "Shots showing the wider view, however, were only revealed later after being obtained by Joseph Farah's G2 Bulletin, the online intelligence newsletter published by WND's founder. The oversized emblem for the conference shows an hourglass with two balls falling through—one representing the U.S., already cracked and fallen, the second representing Israel."[11]

Make no mistake. Ahmadinejad means what he says. For him, the United States and Israel are ready to fall, and the sands in the hourglass are running out. He wants to drive Israel into the sea.

As one can imagine, this kind of talk has triggered a strong response from Israel.

Israeli prime minister Ehud Olmert said, "The Jewish people, with the scars of the Holocaust fresh on its body, cannot afford to allow itself to face threats of annihilation once again."[12] The threat against Israel is so dire that the former chief of the Israeli Mossad intelligence agency, Meir Amit, has called for the assassination of Ahmadinejad. He said, "Ahmadinejad is the pusher of all the Muslim world toward fanaticism and extremism. In his case, he should be made to disappear from the arena. He has said he wants to become a *shahid,* a martyr, so I think he should get his wish and be sent to heaven."[13]

The stage is set for a monumental clash between Israel and Iran. In fact, Ahmadinejad has wasted little time in backing up his words with action. The conflict has already begun with the thirty-four-day Israel-Hezbollah War in the summer of 2006, directed by Iran. Hezbollah, acting as Iran's surrogate and proxy, unleashed a relentless rocket attack on northern Israel. As we've already seen, Hezbollah is basically Iran on Israel's northern border. Israel's war with Hezbollah was "Iran v. Israel, Part 1." Rest assured, there's more to come.

Demonizing the Jews

The second part of Ahmadinejad's anti-Semitic strategy is his consistent and frequent demonizing of the Jews and Israel. There's a major campaign in Iran to accomplish this precondition for genocide.[14] According to the *Middle East Media Research Institute,* Iranian state-controlled television produces numerous television series that depict the Jews in the most unflattering light. Here's a small sample of the propaganda campaign:

> These include classic blood libels, depicting Jews as using the blood of non-Jewish children to bake their Passover matzos, and as kidnapping non-Jewish children to steal

their body parts. Jews are reduced to sub-human levels, depicted as pigs and apes. They are accused of persecuting the Prophet Muhammad in voodoo ritualistic scenes, and as tormenting a historic figure reminiscent of Jesus on the Cross. All these TV series exist alongside others that deny the Holocaust. Again, it should be stressed that all these phenomena are interrelated, and are state-directed at the highest level. It is most indicative that Ahmadinejad's first public appearance after coming to power was made before television producers.[15]

Dehumanizing the Jews makes their elimination much more palatable. Even justifiable.

Denying the Holocaust

Ahmadinejad knows that it would be difficult to muster widespread support for his anti-Semitism as long as the Jews are the object of sympathy for the Holocaust. Therefore, Ahmadinejad must deny that any such event ever occurred, in order to erase the image of the Jews as victims.[16] His Holocaust denial is pervasive. This is the third strand of his anti-Semitic strategy. As Yigal Carmon observes, "In either case, Ahmadinejad's primary obsession is not with the Holocaust, but with Israel's very existence. If the Holocaust gets in the way of achieving this goal, it must be denied."[17]

In response to the Danish newspaper cartoon depicting the

prophet Muhammad as a homicide bomber, an Iranian newspaper, in March 2006, held a contest seeking the best Holocaust-themed cartoon. The cartoons attempted to demonstrate that the Holocaust never happened, or at a minimum was gratuitously exploited by the Jews to support their claims to Palestine.[18] Then, to carry it even further, in December 2006, Ahmadinejad sponsored a meeting of Holocaust deniers from all over the world. David Duke, the former KKK imperial wizard from the United States, even attended the meeting and denied that gas chambers were used to kill millions of Jews.[19]

In response to the Holocaust Denial Conference, on January 26, 2007, the United Nations passed a resolution condemning Holocaust denial. In response to the UN resolution, Hossein Shariatmadari, who is close to the Iranian supreme leader Mohammed Ali Khamenei, attacked the UN and said, "The myth of the Holocaust is an excuse [used by the] West to establish the illegal Zionist regime, and denial of it is an irrefutable attestation—in addition to many other attestations—that clearly testify to the illegality of the existence of the Zionist regime."[20]

Iranian television channel 4 ran a thirteen-part documentary series titled *Merchants of the Myth,* that ran from October 2006 through January 2007. The gist of this Holocaust-denial documentary series was that the entire Holocaust is a myth perpetrated by Zionists and its Western sympathizers. The series featured several notorious Holocaust deniers and historical revisionists.[21]

Ahmadinejad's use of Holocaust denial to repudiate Israel's right to exist can be seen in this statement on October 20, 2006:

"This [Zionist regime] was established in order to shore up the entire region, and to place it at the disposal of the world forces. It is a big lie that it was done in order to protect those killed in World War II, and in order to compensate them. Over 60 million people were killed in World War II. Let's assume you are right, and six million [Jews] were among those killed. How come none of you mourn the other 54 million? Why don't you pay reparations to them? Why don't you ever think about them? All your sorrow, your pity, your mourning cries are over [victims] who were counted by I don't know whom."[22]

On May 28, 2006, in an interview with Germany's *Der Spiegel* magazine, Ahmadinejad said, "We say that if the Holocaust happened, then the Europeans must accept the consequences and the price should not be paid by Palestine. If it did not happen, then the Jews must return to where they came from."[23] In an ironic twist, Ahmadinejad denies the reality of the Holocaust, and yet he wants to repeat it.

Waller R. Newell, professor of political science at Carleton University in Ottawa, makes this powerful observation: "He [Ahmadinejad] does not represent all political forces in Iran, not even all radical forces.... But as long as he is president, Ahmadinejad represents an important dimension of the Iranian revolution we cannot afford to ignore. As long as Iranian policy is dominated by Ahmadinejad and his allies among the senior clerics of the Islamic Republic, Iran cannot be negotiated with. Their commitment to the destruction of the Jews is a matter of principle, just as the implementation of the Holocaust was for the Nazis."[24]

60 MINUTES OF SPIN

Well-known journalist and *60 Minutes* reporter Mike Wallace interviewed Ahmadinejad in the presidential palace in Tehran on August 8, 2006. Here's a transcript of the part of the interview dealing with the president's statements about the destruction of Israel.[25] Ahmadinejad never explained his genocidal comments, but used the opportunity to once again question the reality of the Holocaust.

Wallace began with these comments to set up the interview, which took place while the Israel-Hezbollah War was raging:

Wallace: When Iran's President Mahmoud Ahmadinejad

speaks out candidly, and he does it a lot, he scares a
lot of people. He has said more than once that Israel
should be wiped off the map and that the Holocaust is
an overblown fairy tale. Interviewing him in Tehran this
past week, it became apparent that he sees the fighting
between Israel and Hezbollah, that militia Iran has long
supported, as part of a larger battle between the U.S.
and a militant Islam for control of the Middle East.

Not long into the interview, Wallace brought up the question of Israel:

Wallace: Israel, you have said time and again, Israel must be

wiped off the map. Please explain why, and what is
Iran doing about that?

Ahmadinejad: *(translated throughout)*

Well, allow me to finish with the nuclear dossier first.

Wallace: Oh, you finished with that. You finished with that. Tell me—

Ahmadinejad: No, it's not finished, sir. It's not finished. We are just beginning.

Wallace: Okay. That's what I was afraid of, but go.

Ahmadinejad: Well, the Americans are overly sensitive, and of course the American government. I don't know why they're opposed to Iranian progress.

Wallace: The United States is against Iranian progress and development?

Ahmadinejad: That is true. That is what I am saying.

Wallace: Ah, you know that's not so.

Ahmadinejad: Well, I'm going to explain. Before the revolution, the German, French, American governments and the Canadian government had signed contracts with us to produce nuclear fuel inside Iran, but immediately after the establishment of the Islamic Republic, their opposition started. Right now, they are opposed to our nuclear technology. Now, why is that?

Wallace: Because the U.S. is convinced that nuclear energy is just a smokescreen, that what Iran really wants is the bomb.

Wallace: *(narrating interview)*
Then I tried to get the president back to his most inflammatory statement.

Wallace: You are very good at filibustering. You still have not answered the question. You still have not answered the question: Israel must be wiped off the map. Why?

Ahmadinejad: Well, don't be hasty, sir. I'm going to get to that.

Wallace: I'm not hasty.

Ahmadinejad: I think that the Israeli government is a fabricated government.

Wallace: *(narrating interview)*

Fabricated following the Holocaust, which he has said may also have been fabricated.

Wallace: Last December, you said this: "The Europeans created a myth—the Holocaust." A myth?

Ahmadinejad: What I did say was that if this is a reality, if this is real, where did it take place?

Wallace: In Germany.

Ahmadinejad: There are *(unintelligible)*.

Wallace: In Germany.

Ahmadinejad: Who caused this in Europe?

Wallace: In Europe. What you are suggesting—one moment— what you are suggesting, then, that Israel should be over in Germany because that's where the Holocaust took place?

Ahmadinejad: I'm not saying that, mind you.

Wallace: *(narrating interview)*

But he has said Israel could be moved to Europe or even to the United States, but it should not be in Palestine.

Ahmadinejad: Well, if an atrocity was committed in Germany, or Europe for that matter, why should the Palestinians answer for this? They had no role to play in this. Why on the pretext of the Holocaust they have occupied Palestine? Millions of people have been made refugees. Thousands of people to date have been killed, sir. Thousands of people have been put in prison. Well, at the very moment, a great war is raging because of that.

Throughout the interview, Ahmadinejad's demeanor spoke just as loudly as his words. He smiled and displayed overt arrogance, speaking with cunning evasiveness. He kept his anger under control, but one could easily see that it was boiling just beneath the surface. His venom for the Jewish state was there on open display for all to see.

THE WORLD IS WAKING UP

Fortunately, many world leaders are taking Ahmadinejad seriously. Dead seriously.

Former Israeli prime minister Benjamin Netanyahu said, "In the '30s too no one believed that Hitler was capable of taking action because he didn't explicitly talk about wiping out the Jewish people. In contrast, the Iranian president publicly announces his intentions, and no one is trying to stop him."[26]

In January 2007, Netanyahu visited London and met with Canadian and British members of Parliament to gather their support for his initiative to put Iranian president Mahmoud Ahmadinejad on trial at The Hague for inciting genocide. Some have joined the call and are trying to obtain an international indictment against Ahmadinejad. Calling for war crimes charges against Ahmadinejad, Netanyahu said, "If Israel needs, it will defend itself. But the question is whether the world will protect itself. In the case that Israel is attacked first, those who will be hurt most are the neighboring Arab countries. Therefore, this is an international interest. Today, Ahmadinejad has missiles that can reach Israel, but he wants to reach Paris and London."[27]

In an April 2006 interview, outgoing Israeli minister of defense Shaul Mofaz said, "Of all the threats we face, Iran is the biggest. The world must not wait. We must do everything necessary on a diplomatic level in order to stop its nuclear activity. Since Hitler we have not faced such a threat."[28]

Comparisons to Hitler are not only coming from Israel. Angela Merkel, the German chancellor, has said that Ahmadinejad is a rising Adolf Hitler and poses a similar threat to the world, except that Iran would even be worse if it acquires nuclear weapons. On February 4, 2006, she said, "In the early 1930s when National Socialism [Nazism] was on the rise, there were many who said, 'It's only rhetoric—don't get excited.' Iran has blatantly crossed the red line. We must prevent Iran from developing its nuclear program. A president who questions Israel's right to exist, a president who denies the Holocaust cannot expect to receive any tolerance from Germany."[29]

Newt Gingrich, former Speaker of the House of Representatives, said in January 2006: "This is 1935 and Mahmoud Ahmadinejad is as close to Adolf Hitler as we've seen. We know who they are. The question is, who are we—are we [Stanley] Baldwin or [Winston] Churchill?"[30]

Gingrich is right. Ahmadinejad is very much like Hitler. And that would be terrible enough by itself. But another twist to this story makes it even more chilling. Ahmadinejad is on an apocalyptic quest for nuclear weapons.

Imagine Hitler with the bomb. That's what the Jewish people face if Ahmadinejad's nuclear train is not derailed. Waller R. Newell issues this sober warning:

> Unfortunately, whether mad or not, Ahmadinejad has a coherent ideological vision in which the call to wipe out Israel is no ordinary manifestation of anti-Semitism. Instead, it is the beckoning of an apocalyptic event that will usher in a millennium of bliss for all believers, indeed all mankind. Nuclear weapons are the indispensable means to this end since they are the most reliable way of exterminating the Jewish state. They are therefore not to be negotiated away in exchange for other economic and security benefits. The revolution needs nuclear weapons to carry out its utopian mission."[31]

Ahmadinejad is on the fast track to making his mission a reality.

Five

AHMADINEJAD'S RACE FOR THE NUCLEAR FINISH LINE

We advise them not to play with the lion's tail.... It is too late to stop the progress of Iran.

MAHMOUD AHMADINEJAD

The mullahs are more likely to use these weapons than anyone in the nuclear age.... These are the questions. These are the calculations. The decision is no more than a year away.

CHARLES KRAUTHAMMER
(SEPTEMBER 15, 2006)

When we say we have entered industrial-scale enrichment, [it means] there is no way back.

REZA AQAZADEH, HEAD OF IRAN'S ATOMIC
ENERGY ORGANIZATION

A country that has attained the knowledge and technology of uranium enrichment is only one step away
from producing nuclear weapons.

HOSSEIN SHARIATMADARI, EDITOR OF *KAYHAN*,
A CONSERVATIVE DAILY IRANIAN NEWSPAPER

Yesterday, Iran crossed the nuclear point of no
return. Now it is for all practical purposes a nuclear
state.

EDITORIAL IN *KAYHAN* (APRIL 10, 2007)

Hitler went out on a world campaign first, and then
tried to get nuclear weapons. Iran is trying to get
nuclear arms first. Therefore from that perspective, it
is much more dangerous. Hitler was defeated because
he could not develop weapons of mass destruction.
But Iran stands close to developing nuclear weapons.
Does the world understand?

BENJAMIN NETANYAHU

APPROACHING NUCLEAR MIDNIGHT

Chicago, January 2007. The board of directors of the *Bulletin of the
Atomic Scientists* moved the minute hand of the Doomsday Clock
from seven minutes to five minutes till midnight.[1]

The Doomsday Clock was created in 1947 by the *Bulletin of the Atomic Scientists* as a symbolic measure or gauge of the continuous danger the world faces in the nuclear age. At its inception, the minute hand on the clock was placed at seven minutes to midnight. Since that time the hand has been moved eighteen times. It was closest to midnight—two minutes—in 1953 when the United States and the Soviet Union both tested hydrogen bombs within nine months of each other. It was farthest from midnight in 1991—seventeen minutes—when the United States and the Soviet Union signed the Strategic Arms Reduction Treaty and announced further unilateral cuts in their nuclear weapon stockpiles. Before January 2007, the last time it was moved was in 2002.[2]

The *Bulletin* justified the recent two-minute move based on several key criteria that the directors believe constitute a "deteriorating state of global affairs."

We stand at the brink of a second nuclear age. Not since the first atomic bombs were dropped on Hiroshima and Nagasaki has the world faced such perilous choices. North Korea's recent test of a nuclear weapon, Iran's nuclear ambitions, a renewed U.S. emphasis on the military utility of nuclear weapons, the failure to adequately secure nuclear materials, and the continued presence of some 26,000 nuclear weapons in the United States and Russia are symptomatic of a larger failure to solve the problems posed by the most destructive technology on Earth…. The Clock is ticking.[3]

For the first time in its history, the *Bulletin* included climate change as a factor in its decision. But it went on to say, "Nuclear weapons still pose the most potent threat to humanity."[4] The *Bulletin* makes the frightening case that man has acquired "the power to unmake God's creation…. One way to look at our predicament is to say that we threaten to run Genesis in reverse."[5]

Since 1945 the global "nuclear club" has expanded from one nuclear-capable nation to nine, now that North Korea officially has become the most recent member last year. The *Bulletin* expands on this frightening statistic: "Since 1945, the nuclear club has grown from one to nine, with potentially 20 to 30 more nations and an unknown number of terrorist groups bidding for membership. Numberless fingers on nuclear buttons in a volatile political climate marked by the practice of jihad and suicide bombing makes a holocaust seem highly likely. Doomsday with a bang. Destruction without redemption for the good, the bad, the innocent, and the guilty."[6]

There are currently about 27,000 nuclear weapons in the world. Of these, 26,000 are in the United States (10,000) and Russia (16,000). Each of these warheads has eight to forty times the destructive power of the atomic bomb dropped on Hiroshima. Nuclear theft from Russia is still a major concern among experts. The world is clearly becoming a more dangerous place as each day passes. And little is being done to head off the impending disaster.

The *Bulletin* warns, "The four horsemen of the modern apocalypse are riding roughshod over Earth. The Bomb has already fallen. The stealth apocalypse is well under way, and the advanced nations lack the collective will to do anything about our precarious situation."[7]

CURRENT NUCLEAR ARSENALS[8]	
Country	*Weapons Total*
United States	10,100
Russia	16,000
France	350
Britain	200
China	200
Israel	75–200
India	40–50
Pakistan	24–48

The Final *A* of Ahmadinejad's Apocalypse

As the world stands on the precipice of a nuclear doomsday, of approaching midnight, the nation that poses the greatest threat, if it gets the bomb, is Iran. And the reason goes back to the first two A's in our three-part apocalypse formula. We've looked in some depth at the first two pieces of Ahmadinejad's apocalypse: Apocalyptic ideology and Anti-Semitism. He has flatly stated that his main mission is to usher in the Mahdi. And to bring in the Mahdi, Israel must be destroyed.

On April 14, 2006, Ahmadinejad said, "The Zionist regime is an injustice and by its very nature a permanent threat. Whether you like it or not, the Zionist regime is heading toward annihilation. The Zionist regime is a rotten, dried tree that will be eliminated by one storm." What could eliminate Israel in "one storm"? An atomic bomb. As Alireza Jafarzadeh notes, "With a nuclear arsenal, the Iranian regime can carry out its stated objective of wiping Israel off the map."[9] Also, what could bring in the worldwide chaos and bloodshed that is necessary for the Mahdi's return? Atomic weapons—the final, missing component to Ahmadinejad's apocalypse.

Certainly many in Iran would love to join the nuclear club for all kinds of reasons. To give it international clout and prestige. To boost its nationalistic pride. To give the Shiites a bomb to counteract the "Jewish bomb" in Israel and the "Sunni bomb" in Pakistan. But underlying all these reasons is the apocalyptic ideology of

Ahmadinejad and Supreme Leader Khamenei. The bomb is their final storm to obliterate Israel. Their ticket to utopia. Their pathway to the Mahdi's coming.

And they may be perilously close to getting it.

To help us understand how real and serious the threat is and how we arrived at the current crisis, let's examine Iran's nuclear quest and its driving force, Mahmoud Ahmadinejad—a lethal combination that some have aptly called "Iranium."

IRANIUM

Iran signed the Treaty on the Non-Proliferation of Nuclear Weapons in 1968, which required it to submit all nuclear-related activities to the International Atomic Energy Agency (IAEA). However, beginning in the late 1980s, Iran launched a clandestine nuclear program with the aid of Pakistani scientist Abdul Qadeer Khan. This began a fifteen-year game of nuclear cat and mouse between the IAEA and Iran, in which Iran has consistently denied the existence of any nuclear program. But in August 2002, in the face of irrefutable evidence, the shroud was officially torn away from Iran's violations of the nuclear nonproliferation treaty. The reality of secret nuclear production sites at Natanz and Arak was disclosed for all to see.

With its nuclear program exposed, Iran agreed to suspend any nuclear-enrichment activities, and all was well for over three years. But that changed very quickly when Ahmadinejad assumed the presidency.

Some experts believe that Iran today may have as many as three hundred nuclear sites or facilities. In fact, on May 14, 2007, the *New York Times* gave this sobering report about Iran's progress in its nuclear program.

> Inspectors for the International Atomic Energy Agency have concluded that Iran appears to have solved most of its technological problems and is now beginning to enrich uranium on a far larger scale than before, according to the agency's top officials....

The *Times* went on to give the rest of the bad news.

> According to diplomats familiar with the inspectors' report,...at this pace, Iran could have 3,000 centrifuges operating by June—enough to make one bomb's worth of material every year.[10]

There are varying estimates of how long it will take for Iran to produce a nuclear bomb, but David Albright, a former nuclear inspector, said on May 15, 2007, that he believes Iran is about two years from producing a nuclear weapon, should it choose to do so.

IRAN'S NUCLEAR NETWORK[11]

- *Natanz:* An enormous, sprawling nuclear-enrichment facility that includes a centrifuge pilot plant in operation since January 2006. The plant is half the size of the Pentagon. The two underground centrifuge cascade halls could ultimately hold over fifty thousand centrifuges.

- *Arak:* The heavy-water production plant, operational since August 2006, and a heavy-water nuclear reactor under construction are capable of producing plutonium (the second route to production of nuclear weapons).
- *Kalaye Electric Company in Tehran:* A centrifuge testing facility.
- *Lavizan-Shian:* The nuclear facility there was destroyed allegedly to hide evidence from the IAEA.
- *Lavizan 2:* A laser-enrichment facility, built with equipment from the Lavizan-Shian site. It is off-limits to the IAEA.
- *Bushehr:* A civilian nuclear reactor being built with Russian help.
- *Isfahan:* A huge uranium conversion facility used to convert uranium "yellowcake" into uranium hexafluoride, the feedstock for centrifuges.
- *Tehran:* Extensive tunnels and hardened underground bunker sites to hide the nuclear-weapons program and missiles.
- *Military Complexes:* Widespread use for nuclear-weapons research and development.
- *National Universities:* Widespread use for nuclear-weapons research and development.

- *Secret Company in Tehran:* Produces P-1 (aluminum rotor) and P-2 (steel rotor) centrifuges for uranium enrichment (P stands for Pakistan). P-2 centrifuges enrich uranium much faster than P-1. Ahmadinejad has boasted that Iran already has P-2 centrifuges in use.

AHMADINEJAD AND THE NUCLEAR FAST TRACK

Iran's undeterrable quest for the bomb has been evident from the outset of Ahmadinejad's presidency. And even before. In July 2005, before he was even sworn in as president, Ahmadinejad paid a visit to the uranium enrichment facility at Natanz.[12] This was a chilling omen of things to come. A nuclear Iran is the centerpiece of his presidency.

On Ahmadinejad's inauguration day, August 6, 2005, Tehran formally announced that it was rejecting the offer from the EU-3 (Britain, France, and Germany) to help develop Iran's nuclear-power program.[13] Only two days after his inauguration, the government resumed uranium conversion at its Isfahan plant in direct violation of its November 2006 agreement with the EU-3. Also, soon after his inauguration, Ahmadinejad named a new chief nuclear negotiator, Ali Larijani, "a former senior commander of the Islamic Revolutionary Guards Corps and prominent hard-line conservative with close ties to Khomeini."[14]

Then on January 10, 2006, Ahmadinejad ordered the removal of the seals from the uranium-enrichment facility at Natanz. This began what has become a tiresome charade as Ahmadinejad has repeatedly defied and even taunted the UN Security Council and the West.

The first major test of wills came in the summer of 2006. UN Resolution 1696 (June 31, 2006) offered multiple economic incentives to Iran to suspend its nuclear-enrichment program. Iran was given until August 31 to respond. Interestingly, Ahmadinejad chose August 22, 2006, nine days early, as the date to thumb his nose at the United Nations. Why this date?

In the Islamic calendar, August 22 is the date of the famous "night flight" by the Prophet Muhammad on his faithful steed from Saudi Arabia to the Temple Mount in Jerusalem, and then to heaven and back again. This date is often associated with the apocalyptic return of the Hidden Imam or Mahdi. It's also the date on which Saladin conquered Jerusalem. Therefore, for Ahmadinejad, this date carries both religious and political importance.[15] This is another example of how Ahmadinejad's end-time ideology and nuclear pursuit are part and parcel of one overarching apocalyptic scheme.

On August 24, just one week before the August 31 deadline, "Iran began enriching a new batch of uranium in the 164-machine cascade at Natanz."[16] And in another act of open, calculated defiance, on August 26, "Ahmadinejad inaugurated the heavy-water production plant in Arak."[17]

On December 23, 2006, the UN Security Council issued Resolution 1737, which gave Iran until February 23, 2007, to respond and threatened mild economic sanctions for failure to suspend nuclear enrichment.

For a second time, Ahmadinejad defiantly refused to submit to the UN Security Council's demands. He even called the resolutions "trash paper." Iran has missed one deadline after another. But the United Nations presses on with the weakest penalties possible, due in great part to Russian and Chinese failure to support any sanctions with real teeth. The Iran Policy Committee draws this interesting analogy: "The situation at the UN Security Council is reminiscent of the Aesop fable in which a committee of mice decide they would be well-served by placing a bell around the neck of the cat who preys on them. However, no single mouse can muster the courage to 'bell the cat.' Similarly, the UN Security Council has been unable to impose any but the weakest penalties for Iranian nuclear noncompliance."[18]

THE NUCLEAR LEAP

The January 10, 2006, resumption of operations at Natanz officially began Iran's race for the nuclear finish line. The country rounded the first turn in the race on April 9, 2006, when Ahmadinejad boldly announced to the world that it had enriched uranium at a pilot plant.

On the one-year anniversary of the beginning of nuclear enrichment (April 9, 2007), Ahmadinejad appeared at a ceremony at the Natanz facility held in honor of National Day for Nuclear Technology, which apparently is the new designation for April 9.

Standing in front of an Iranian flag bearing the atomic symbol, he declared that his country is now capable of producing enriched uranium on an "industrial scale." He said, "I am proud to say that right from today our country has entered the group of countries that produce nuclear fuel industrially.... The Iranian people have reached the stage of nuclear industrial production and Iran has thus joined the club of great nuclear states. This great achievement has been realized, with dependence on local potentials."[19] He added that this step was, "a dream come true for Iranians all over the world." He also repeated his frequent statement that nuclear power is Iran's "inalienable right" and that the path is "irreversible."[20]

Ahmadinejad never specified the scale of the enrichment, but Iran's nuclear negotiator confirmed that uranium gas was being fed into 3,000 centrifuges. This was the first step toward the stated goal of 54,000 centrifuges. According to David Albright of the Institute for Science and International Security in Washington DC, about 1,500 centrifuges spinning nonstop for one year can produce twenty-eight kilograms (sixty-two pounds) of the 90 percent enriched uranium needed to construct a nuclear bomb. Albright added that such enrichment "would escalate the confrontation," and said, "It raises all kinds of worst-case scenarios that, if not managed correctly could escalate up to a military action."[21] It now appears that Iran is rounding the corner for the homestretch in its race for the bomb. Mark Fitzpatrick of the International Institute for Strategic Studies in London told the BBC that the Iranians "have passed some kind of threshold."

Ahmadinejad also added this stern warning to anyone who interferes with Iran's nuclear quest: "They should know that our nation with awareness and faith has stood by its leadership and will defend its rights to the end." He also added, "The Iranian people will not allow the arrogant powers to stop their scientific march and will proceed with it till reaching the peaks in the scientific research." He called on Western powers to recognize Tehran's right to nuclear power and refrain from "fruitless intransigence." Ahmadinejad's proclamation was a direct challenge to the UN Security Council. On March 24, 2007, the council gave Iran sixty days to suspend enrichment. But this was after Iran thumbed its nose at three previous deadlines. Ahmadinejad also restated his commitment to help other states "attain their NPT [Non-Proliferation Treaty] rights."[22]

According to *Gulf Daily News,* on April 9, 2007, "Across Iran, school bells rang to mark the 'national day of nuclear energy.' The government sent out text messages of congratulation for the occasion to millions of mobile phone users. In Tehran, some two hundred students formed a human death chain at Iran's Atomic Energy Organization while chanting 'death to America' and 'death to Britain.'"[23]

Also on that same day, Iran's supreme leader Ayatollah Khamenei said that Iran's nuclear program was more important to the nation than the nationalization of oil in 1958.[24] This made publicly evident Iran's utter devotion to its nuclear program. Khamenei then added a threat of his own: "If they want to treat us with threats and use force or violence, the Iranian nation will undoubtedly use all its capabilities to strike the invading enemies."[25]

In response to Ahmadinejad's announcement, the White House said it is "very concerned" and that Iran's actions are "unacceptable." One can be sure that this announcement has caused shock waves in Israel, which knows full well that Iran is the greatest threat to its continued existence.

AHMADINEJAD'S "BOMBS"

Ahmadinejad has fired off hundreds of verbal salvos over the nuclear issue. His inflammatory speeches have made his intentions crystal clear. Here are just a few samples of his nuclear "bombs":[26]

- "We know well that a country's backing down one iota on its undeniable rights is the same as losing everything. We will not bend to a few countries' threats."

- "The Iranian people are standing firm until the end on acquiring their right and will not shift an inch. The Iranian nation will not be dissuaded in its drive, and the Iranian nation stands united on this. On the nuclear issue, the Iranian people will stand firm to acquire all their rights, will continue solidly to reach the summits of perfection, and will raise their fists to insist on their rights."[27]

- "A country, which possesses the biggest nuclear arsenal, embarks on proliferation of nuclear weapons in defiance of the safeguards and threatens to use them against others, is not competent to comment on peaceful use of nuclear know-how by other states."

- In a threat to play the oil card, Ahmadinejad said, "If Iran's nuclear case is referred to the Security Council of the United Nations, then the response of this country will be to use different ways to stop selling oil."

- "Iran…is ready to transfer atomic knowledge for energy usage to other Islamic countries."

- He referred to Iran's nuclear program as "a flood which cannot be stopped by a match stick. It's impossible to stop a nation's scientific progress with a bunch of irrelevant words…. It would be suicidal for a country to attack Iran…so we must not bend to threats."

- "The West wants to frighten us with the Security Council like little children before a spider. Be angry with us, and from this anger die."

- "The Iranian government and nation has no fear of the Western ballyhoo and will continue its nuclear programs with decisiveness and wisdom."

- Warning that further UN sanctions and resolutions will only accelerate Iran's nuclear program, Ahmadinejad said, "After the first resolution, we undertook the nuclear fuel cycle; after the second one, we began the industrial phase of nuclear fuel; and if another resolution is issued, new capabilities of the Iranian nation will surface."[28]

- Lashing out at the IAEA and UN Security Council for passing a resolution against Iran, he said, "The foes cannot do a damn thing. We do not need you at all. It is you who need the Iranian people.... You can issue as many resolutions as you like and dream on. But you cannot prevent the Iranian nation's progress."

- "In the nuclear case we are ready to take the final step and I hope that by the end of the year [Iranian year to March 2007] we will be able to hold the great celebration of Iran's nuclear right."[29]

- On March 2, 2007, Ahmadinejad likened Iran's nuclear program to a runaway train: "Iran has obtained the technology to produce nuclear fuel and Iran's move is like a nuclear train that has no brakes or reverse gear, because in the past year we have discarded them."[30]

- On April 20, 2007, he said, "Iran has entered the nuclear club and [the West] should accept it. There is no reason to go backwards.... The era of threatening with bombs and missiles is over especially for those who think they can speak with Iran with the language of pressure. We are not a threat to anyone."[31]

These statements unveil Ahmadinejad's unwavering commitment to get his hands on the bomb at all costs, ultimately to fulfill his goals for the Islamic Republic.

NUCLEAR CARTOONS

As evidence of the extent of Ahmadinejad's obsession with Iran's nuclear program, Iran is now making nuclear cartoons. That's right, animation has gone atomic. An animated film aired on Tehran television on February 21, 2007, showing the successful completion of nuclear plants in several Iranian cities by 2022–23. In the cartoons, according to the *Middle East Media Research Institute,* the United States, encouraged by Israel, mobilizes the world's nations to stop the Iranian efforts, but fails.[34] In this cartoon, Iran is the hero and the United States is the villain. This serves as another example of Iranian chest-beating at the expense of the West.

This is one cartoon that's no laughing matter.

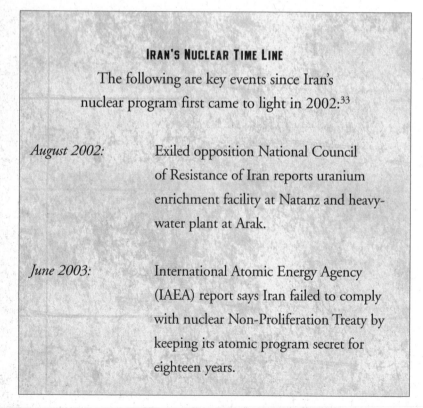

IRAN'S NUCLEAR TIME LINE

The following are key events since Iran's nuclear program first came to light in 2002:[33]

August 2002:	Exiled opposition National Council of Resistance of Iran reports uranium enrichment facility at Natanz and heavy-water plant at Arak.
June 2003:	International Atomic Energy Agency (IAEA) report says Iran failed to comply with nuclear Non-Proliferation Treaty by keeping its atomic program secret for eighteen years.

December 2003:	Iran signs protocol allowing snap inspections of nuclear facilities.
February 2005:	President Mohammed Khatami says no Iranian government will give up nuclear-technology program.
July 2005:	Before he was even sworn in as president, Ahmadinejad paid a visit to the uranium-enrichment facility at Natanz.
September 2, 2005:	IAEA report confirms Iran has resumed uranium conversion at Isfahan.
January 10, 2006:	Iran removes UN seals at Natanz enrichment plant and resumes nuclear-fuel research.
February 4, 2006:	IAEA votes to report Iran to UN Security Council. Iran ends UN snap inspections the next day. Iran restarts small-scale uranium enrichment ten days later.
March 8, 2006:	IAEA report to Security Council says it cannot verify Iran's atomic activities are peaceful.

(continued on next page)

April 11, 2006:	Iran says it has produced low-grade enriched uranium suitable for use in power stations; IAEA confirms this.
April 13, 2006:	Ahmadinejad boasted that Iran was conducting research on the more advanced P-2 centrifuge.
April 28, 2006:	IAEA report to the Security Council confirms Iran has flouted council demands to suspend enrichment.
July 31, 2006:	Security Council demands Iran suspend nuclear activities by August 31. Council makes first legally binding demands in resolution and threatens sanctions.
August 31, 2006:	IAEA announces Iran has not met deadline to suspend program and has resumed enriching uranium.
September 15, 2006:	Alireza Jafarzadeh, the man who brought Iran's nuclear program out into the light in 2003, warned that Iran may have a laser-

enrichment program at Lashkar Ab'ad, which is about fifteen miles northwest of Tehran. He claimed that "the laser enrichment is being conducted under the guise of a front company called Paya Partov whose board is led by Reza Aqazadeh, head of the Atomic Energy Organization of Iran."

September 26, 2006: Russia and Iran agree on start-up date of September 2007 for Iran's first nuclear power station at Bushehr.

November 14, 2006: IAEA report says Iran has started experimental chain of 164 linked centrifuges, feeding uranium gas into them for enrichment.

December 23, 2006: Security Council votes for sanctions and gives sixty days to suspend enrichment. Iran calls the resolution illegal.

January 22, 2007: Iran bars entry to thirty-eight IAEA inspectors after hard-liners demand retaliation for sanctions.

(continued on next page)

February 4, 2007:	Reports from Iran hint of accelerated nuclear activity and claim that Iran needs just one more step in its nuclear program that "will force the world to treat it as it wants."
February 20, 2007:	The Iranian news agency Aftab reports that nine tons of UF6 gas had been transferred from Isfahan to the nuclear facility at Natanz and that, if these nine tons were enriched, it would be possible from them to produce one atom bomb.
February 21, 2007:	A sixty-day grace period to stop enrichment expires.
February 22, 2007:	IAEA says Iran has installed two cascades of 164 centrifuges in Natanz with another two almost completed. These cascades represent efforts to expand research-level enrichment of nuclear fuel into "industrial scale" production.
March 14, 2007:	U.S., British, French, German, Russian, and Chinese diplomats at the United

Nations reach a tentative deal on imposing fresh sanctions. President Mahmoud Ahmadinejad dismisses any new sanctions resolution the next day as "a torn piece of paper."

March 24, 2007:   The Security Council unanimously approves new arms and financial sanctions against Iran for refusing to suspend uranium enrichment.

April 9, 2007:   Iran says it has begun the "industrial stage" of nuclear-fuel production with mass production of uranium-enrichment centrifuges and the launch of industrial-scale enrichment.

April 2007:   Iran moves closer to joining the space race and putting satellites into orbit. Tehran announces that a launch will take place "soon." This breakthrough could give it the ability to fire inter-continental ballistic missiles within a few years.[34]

ATOMIC AYATOLLAHS

Ahmadinejad has made it clear that it is the country's supreme leader, Ayatollah Mohammed Ali Khamenei, not himself, who is ultimately responsible for decisions concerning Tehran's controversial nuclear activities. "The state's major policies on the nuclear issue are decreed by the Supreme Leader. The government is obliged to carry them out and is the entity for making announcements on this matter."[35] Ahmadinejad clarified that he himself was responsible for "announcing" the country's positions. It's kind of like the Emperor and Darth Vader in *Star Wars*. The Ayatollah Khamenei is like the sinister Emperor who lurks in the shadows but really pulls the strings. He's the "master puppeteer."[36] Ahmadinejad is like the evil Darth Vader—the powerful henchman who willingly, eagerly carries out the Emperor's directives. Ahmadinejad is the passionate front man for the Shiite dream.

In any event, Ahmadinejad's comments indicate that his frequent heavy-toned remarks over the nuclear issue are not mere posturing; they are official state policy.[37] This means that even if Ahmadinejad were removed from office, the current nuclear policy in Iran would continue.

"TALK AND BUILD"—THE STRATEGY IS WORKING

So far, Iran's nuclear strategy is working to a tee. While there is some economic unrest back home in Iran, the world appears paralyzed to take any real action. Iran watched as Iraq violated seventeen UN resolutions with impunity. They have watched North Korea cross the nuclear finish line. They know that time is on their side. They are masters at manipulating the international diplomatic community for their advantage.

Alireza Jafarzadeh, author of *The Iran Threat,* provides an excellent summary of the strategy and progress of Iran's nuclear achievements since Ahmadinejad assumed power in August 2005.

> In terms of the nuclear agenda, Ahmadinejad managed to speed up the nuclear weapons program while prolonging negotiations in order to buy more time to advance the regime's nuclear goals. In spite of international pressure, the strides in Iran's uranium enrichment program during this period included the resumption of uranium conversion at the Isfahan facility in August 2005 and of research and development at Natanz in January 2006, accelerated construction of the two large underground cascade halls at Natanz, the enrichment of uranium to nearly five percent in June 2006, stepped-up development of P-2 centrifuges, completion of construction phases at the heavy-water production plant, sped-up completion of the heavy water reactor in Arak, the restart of laser enrichment at Lashkar Ab'ad. Nuclear negotiators during Ahmadinejad's tenure were drawn out by Iran providing vague responses to IAEA and other international inquiries, which instigated further questioning for clarification; repeatedly building false expectations of Iran's willingness to negotiate, only to refuse

such options later; and exploiting Iran-friendly Security Council members Russia and China in order to slow negotiations and postpone sanctions.[38]

Jafarzadeh then offers this conclusion: "Analyzing the presidency of Ahmadinejad demonstrates how nothing has prevented the Iranian regime from stepping up the pace of its nuclear program. The regime's handpicked new president gave the program the benefits of no-holds-barred rhetoric, a hard-line chief nuclear negotiator, and a cabinet dominated by the Islamic Revolutionary Guards Corps—the perfect combination for the final leg of its race to the bomb."[39]

The perfect combination indeed. But a deadly one.

ATOMIC BANKNOTES—"IN NUKES WE TRUST"

Anyone who doubts Iran's determination to perfect the uranium enrichment cycle had better think again. Iran has now put its money where its mouth is. Literally.

In yet another act of defiance and bravado, and as a direct snub to the UN Security Council, the Islamic Republic of Iran introduced a new banknote that carries the atomic symbol. The new banknote was issued on March 12, 2007.

The United States has repeatedly accused Iran of operating a secret nuclear-weapons program. Iran has denied this, maintaining that its only aim is the production of nuclear energy for peaceful purposes. The UN Security Council has imposed economic sanctions on Iran for defying its call to stop uranium enrichment, but Iran insists it has the absolute right to implement a nuclear program.

To demonstrate its defiant determination to see the program through to its conclusion, Iran has published its intention on paper. Iran's colorful new "atomic banknote" is a 50,000-rial note. It shows electrons in orbit around a giant atomic nucleus, super-imposed on a map of Iran. National symbols placed on currency carry great significance for any nation. Many view this as a power-ful demonstration of Iran's pride in its nuclear program. Six mil-lion of the notes were circulated through state banks, according to Iranian officials.

The new note displays more than the atomic symbol. It also bears a prophecy from the Prophet Muhammad: "Men from the land of Persia will attain scientific knowledge even if it is as far as the Pleiades." The Pleiades is a cluster of six stars in the constella-tion Taurus. On the other side of the note there's an image of the late Ayatollah Khomeini, the leader of the 1979 Islamic Revolu-tion in Iran. This is a masterful ploy by the Ahmadinejad regime. Every 50,000-rial note bears the atomic symbol with the "support" of both Muhammad and the ayatollah, the two great spiritual lead-ers of Iran. With this validation, Iran is sending the world its final answer on the nuclear issue. Iran will not back down.

It's interesting that the new 50,000-rial note is worth about $5.40, which is more than double the amount of Iran's previous highest denomination. Many economic experts believe that this is further evidence of Iran's problems with rapid inflation. Iranian officials allege that the inflation rate last year was cut from 14.5 to

10.5 percent. However, sources outside the government say that the actual inflation rate is closer to 16 percent. Domestic issues have plagued the regime of Iranian president Mahmoud Ahmadinejad and caused him to suffer serious setbacks in the December 2006 elections. However, he appears to be weathering the political storm and pressing forward to get the bomb. Within one week of this writing, Ahmadinejad expressed his desire to address the Security Council on the nuclear issue.

Around the time that Iran issued its new nuclear note, Dr. Victor Davis Hanson, a policy adviser to President Bush and a senior fellow at Stanford University's Hoover Institution, was interviewed by the *Jerusalem Post*. When asked about Iran's nuclear program, Hanson said, "I believe we have one to two years, a little more at best."[40] Iran's messianic menace could soon have his hands on a nuclear weapon. And the atomic symbol on Iran's money will become a terrifying reality. It appears that Iran is poised to become the Middle Eastern superpower the Bible predicts in Ezekiel 38:5.

How Long Until a Preemptive Strike?

Both the United States and Israel have stated publicly and repeatedly that they will not allow Iran to obtain nuclear weapons. The U.S. Fifth Fleet has been stationed in the Persian Gulf with two naval battle groups, each headed by a carrier (*John C. Stennis* and *Dwight D. Eisenhower*). On April 2, 2007, the carrier USS *Nimitz* embarked for the Persian Gulf to replace the *Dwight D. Eisenhower*. Naval forces are ramped up in the Gulf. The stage is set for a showdown. Israel, the United States, and Britain, especially in light of its recent humiliation by Iran, cannot allow Tehran to violate UN sanctions with impunity and cross the nuclear finish line. Ahmadinejad is enough of a menace with conventional weapons. If Iran's ayatollahs go atomic, the world will be changed. Forever.

It seems now that it's only a matter of time until Israel or the United States acts preemptively to take out, or at least severely damage, Iran's nuclear megaplex. Both the United States and Israel are on record that they will not allow Iran to get the bomb. In January 2007, Graham Allison, an international affairs professor at Harvard and former Department of Defense official, put the odds at 20 percent that the United States or Israel will bomb Iran's nuclear sites within the next two years.[41]

But in order for Israel to carry out these surgical strikes, it must first receive permission from the United States to fly over Iraqi airspace, since Iraq lies between Israel and Iran. According to a senior Israeli defense official, negotiations are currently underway between Israel and the United States. If successful, the U.S.-led coalition in Iraq will supply an air corridor in the event that Israel determines a unilateral, preemptive military strike is necessary to prevent Iran from building a nuclear weapon. The unnamed official said, "We are planning for every eventuality, and sorting out issues such as these are crucially important. The only way to do this is to fly through US-controlled air space. If we don't sort these issues out now we could have a situation where American and Israeli warplanes start shooting at each other."[42]

According to Con Coughlin in Tel Aviv,

The pace of military planning in Israel has accelerated markedly since the start of this year after Mossad, the Israeli intelligence service, provided a stark intelligence assessment that Iran, given the current rate of progress being made on its uranium enrichment programme, could have enough fissile material for a nuclear warhead by 2009. Last week Ehud Olmert, the Israeli prime minister, announced that he had persuaded Meir Dagan, the head of Mossad for the past six years and one of Israel's leading experts on Iran's nuclear programme, to defer his retirement until at least the end of next year. Mr. Olmert has also given overall control of the military aspects of the Iran issue to Eliezer Shkedi, the head of the Israeli Air Force and a former F-16 fighter pilot.[43]

While Israeli officials publicly deny that they are seeking this permission, it makes sense that Israel would remove this initial impediment as it develops a strategic plan to halt Iran's nuclear quest. If the world allows Iran to continue to "talk and build" without any crippling consequences, Israel will be forced to act, possibly very soon. And if Israel acts, Iran will unleash its surrogate, Hezbollah, against Israel and will provide it with all the firepower it needs to inflict untold harm on the Jewish state. This could force the United States to step in, as well as other Arab nations, and possibly Russia. An Israeli attack against Iran could push the world to the brink of World War III and set the stage for the Battle of Gog and Magog predicted in Ezekiel 38–39.

TEHRAN'S TWO CLOCKS

In his excellent book *The Persian Puzzle,* Kenneth Pollack provides this insightful analysis about the current time table in the nuclear showdown with Iran.

> Right now, there are two clocks ticking in Tehran. The first is the clock of regime change. Given the sentiments of the people, it seems likely that there will be further meaningful change in Iran at some point in the future. The second clock is the clock of Iran's nuclear program. We do not know when the alarm on either of those clocks will go off. History has demonstrated that meaningful change in Iran is likely to take considerable time…the findings of the IAEA suggest that Iran is getting fairly close to having a fully self-contained enrichment process, if not actual weapons.[44]

Which alarm will sound first? No one knows. But it appears right now that the nuclear clock has the upper hand. And if it does, Ahmadinejad and the mullah regime will have the final piece of its apocalypse strategy in place. They will have what they need to attempt to fulfill their eschatological vision.

But, thankfully, there's one more clock we must never forget. God's clock. The God of heaven and earth has a plan that He is working out, and He has a time table. His clock is the only one that really matters. And the alarm may be set to go off very soon.

Six

THE APOCALYPSE OF JESUS CHRIST

> The Revelation [apocalypse] of Jesus Christ, which
> God gave Him to show to His bond-servants, the
> things which must soon take place.
>
> REVELATION 1:1

We've spent quite a bit of time exploring the apocalypse of Ahmadinejad and what it may mean for the world. It's his utopian vision of how our world will end. What many people may not know is that there's an entire book of the Bible called the "Apocalypse." We know it as the book of Revelation. The final book in the New Testament. Most accurately, though, the title of the book is the Revelation (*apokalupsis*) of Jesus Christ—the Apocalypse of Jesus Christ. The Greek word *apokalupsis* means an unveiling or a removal of the cover from something. In this book, Jesus unveils or takes the cover off the future and reveals how history will climax and what will happen in the final years of this age. It's His apocalypse—the definitive, official version.

Revelation 1:7 gives the theme of the book of Revelation: "Behold, He is coming with the clouds, and every eye will see

Him, even those who pierced Him; and all the tribes of the earth will mourn over Him." I believe that all of Revelation 4–22 is still in the future. Revelation 4–19 graphically depicts the birth pangs of the time of great tribulation that will precede the greatest event in human history—the second coming of Jesus Christ back to planet earth to rule and reign. Revelation 20–22 pictures the thousand-year reign of Jesus, the final satanic rebellion against Christ, the final

KEY SIMILARITIES BETWEEN SHIITE ESCHATOLOGY AND BIBLICAL ESCHATOLOGY	
Twelver End-Time Scenario	*Biblical End-Time Scenario*[1]
There are general and specific signs of the Mahdi's return.	There are general and specific signs of Jesus's return (Matthew 24).
Antichrist figure (Dajaal).	Antichrist (1 John 2:18, 22; Revelation 13:1–10).
Coming of the Mahdi preceded by time of great tribulation.	Coming of Jesus preceded by time of great tribulation (Matthew 24:21).

judgment, and the eternal state with a new heaven and a new earth and the dwelling place of God among men.

Throughout the book of Revelation, the scene shifts back and forth several times from heaven to earth. This shows that what is occurring on earth is being controlled by God from His throne in heaven. God is the supreme sovereign over the universe. He's in total control. There's no greater comfort than this in troubled times.

At the Mahdi's coming, a voice from heaven, the angel Gabriel.	At Christ's coming, a voice from heaven, the archangel Michael (1 Thessalonians 4:17).
Battle of Gog and Magog (Yajooj and Majooj).	Battle of Gog and Magog (Ezekiel 38–39).
Mahdi returns and rules for seven years.	Jesus returns and rules for a thousand years (Revelation 19:11–20:6).
The world will enjoy prosperity, peace, and justice.	The world will enjoy prosperity, peace, and justice.
Followers believe the coming of the Mahdi is very near.	Followers believe the coming of Christ is near.

COMPETING ESCHATOLOGIES

As we have examined Ahmadinejad's apocalypse, those who know something about the end-time scenario in the Bible may have noted some conspicuous parallels and certainly some major differences between the two. This shouldn't surprise us. Muhammad composed the Koran about five hundred years after the final book of the Bible was written. Some of its history resembles the Old Testament narratives. And some of its prophecy bears similarity too. The charts in this chapter summarize some of the key similarities and differences between these two views of future history-concluding events.

IMPORTANT DIFFERENCES BETWEEN SHIITE ESCHATOLOGY AND BIBLICAL ESCHATOLOGY	
Twelver End-Time Scenario	*Biblical End-Time Scenario*
The Mahdi returns as the focus. Jesus is simply his deputy.	Jesus returns as King of kings and Lord of lords to rule the earth (Revelation 19:11–21).
All must convert to Islam.	All must acknowledge Jesus's lordship.
Followers can accelerate the Mahdi's coming.	The time of Jesus's coming is set by God.

MAHDI AND ANTICHRIST

One difficult, but interesting, aspect of the comparison between the two apocalypses has to do with the several striking similarities between the Islamic Mahdi and the biblical Antichrist. These similarities have caused some to wonder if this may lead many Muslims to unknowingly accept the Antichrist when he appears on earth. Others have theorized that the future Antichrist predicted in the Bible may be a Muslim. While this is possible, it is highly unlikely

SIMILARITIES BETWEEN THE MAHDI AND THE ANTICHRIST	
Mahdi rules the world for seven years.	Antichrist rules for seven years before Jesus comes (Daniel 9:27).
Mahdi persecutes the Jews.	Antichrist befriends the Jews and then, in one of the great double-crosses of all time, breaks his treaty and mercilessly persecutes them.
Mahdi rules the world from Kufa, Iraq (about one hundred miles south of Baghdad).	Antichrist rules the world from Babylon, Iraq (fifty miles south of Baghdad) (Revelation 17–18).

that a Muslim could claim to be a god and be accepted by other Muslims, since the major tenet of Islam is that there is one god, Allah. A man claiming to be Allah in human flesh probably wouldn't get far with Muslims. In any event, this chart presents some correspondences between the Islamic Mahdi and the biblical Antichrist.

CAN WE KNOW FOR SURE?

How can we know which one of these competing eschatologies is true? Is it the apocalypse of Ahmadinejad or the Apocalypse of Jesus? Is there any way to be certain what the future holds? Is there a reliable guide?

I believe that the only way to know which of these apocalypses is true is to ask a very simple question: Which view of the future has a proven track record we can examine? The answer is clear. Only the Bible. In fact, the God of the Bible is so certain that only He can accurately predict the future that He throws down the gauntlet and challenges any other so-called god to tell the future:

Let them bring forth and declare to us what is going to
    take place;
As for the former events, declare what they were,
That we may consider them and know their outcome.
Or announce to us what is coming;
Declare the things that are going to come afterward,
That we may know that you are gods;

Indeed, do good or evil, that we may anxiously look about
   us and fear together. (Isaiah 41:22–23)

Who is like Me? Let him proclaim and declare it;
Yes, let him recount it to Me in order,
From the time that I established the ancient nation.
And let them declare to them the things that are coming
And the events that are going to take place. (Isaiah 44:7)

Only God can tell the future because only God is omniscient
(knows all) and omnipotent (controls all). He has proved it time
and time again. Consider this list, which is far from exhaustive, of
some of the biblical prophecies that have already been fulfilled pre-
cisely as predicted.

What are the odds of even one of these prophecies being fulfilled? And these are just ten of the hundreds of biblical prophecies
that could be cited. Experts claim that there are about three hundred Old Testament prophecies that were fulfilled just in the first
coming of Christ. The odds of one person coincidentally fulfilling
just eight of these is ten to the seventeenth power. That's a one with
eighteen zeros after it. Since a number that large is difficult for us
to imagine, consider this simple illustration. Suppose you took the
state of Texas and spread silver dollars two feet deep across the
whole state, then marked just one of them and buried it somewhere in the state. Then if you chose one person, blindfolded him,
and told him to pick just one silver dollar, his chances of getting

TEN FULFILLED BIBLICAL PROPHECIES

Prophecy	Written or Stated	Fulfilled
Genesis 49:10 Messiah will be from the tribe of Judah.	ca. 1440 BC	5 BC
Isaiah 53 The death of the Messiah	ca. 700 BC	AD 33
Daniel 2 and 7 Gentile world empires in succession (Babylon, Medo-Persia, Greece, Rome, and a reunited Roman Empire)	ca. 530 BC	Throughout history, beginning in 605 BC—to be continued in the end times.
Daniel 9:24–26 483 years after a decree to restore and rebuild Jerusalem, Messiah the Prince will come.	ca. 530 BC	March 30, AD 33, Triumphal Entry, (173,880 days from March 5, 444 BC to March 30, AD 33, fulfilled to the very day).

Isaiah 7:14 Messiah born of a virgin.	ca. 700 BC	5 BC
Micah 5:2 Messiah born in Bethlehem.	ca. 700 BC	5 BC
Isaiah 40:3 Messiah preceded by a messenger.	ca. 700 BC	AD 30
Zechariah 9:9 Messiah will enter Jerusalem riding on a donkey.	ca. 520 BC	AD 33
Matthew 24:1–3 Jesus prophesied the Temple would be destroyed.	AD 33	AD 70
Matthew 24:9, 14 Jesus prophesied that his following would be a world-wide movement that would experience persecution.	AD 33	Throughout the current age.

the marked one on his first try would be one in ten to the seventeenth power.[2]

That's just eight prophecies about Jesus. If we added in the hundreds of other fulfilled prophecies, the number would be staggering. Needless to say, the Bible has an unrivaled track record. No other book even comes close. No other book *claims* to come close. Fulfilled prophecy proves the veracity and reliability of the Bible. It also proves that the prophecies that have yet to be fulfilled will be fulfilled exactly as the Bible says.

So what are the biblical prophecies that relate to Iran and the Middle East? And what does the Bible say will happen?

Are There Any Signs?

It's important to bear in mind that events we see today are not yet the fulfillment of Bible prophecy. The curtain has not yet risen on the final act of God's great drama for this current age. The house lights have not yet dimmed, but we can still recognize activity taking place behind the curtain. At present, God is arranging the scenery in its proper place and allowing the actors to assume their positions on the world stage. When everything is in place, God Himself will raise the curtain.

As we observe and evaluate current events, we all want to know what, if any, role they might be playing in setting the stage for the end-time events prophesied in the Bible. At the same time, we must be careful to remember that only God knows the future. We must always evaluate current events in light of the Bible and never the other way around. Also, we need to remember that regardless of how much our present time may appear to fit the biblical template, there may be more development to come. Nevertheless, we need to know and understand biblical prophecy in order to more wisely discern the role of current world events in shaping the future.

I believe current events in Iran and the Middle East are part of the stage setting for the end-time drama. We are witnessing a growing alliance of Muslim nations and Russia that is strikingly similar to the group of nations that will swoop down to invade Israel in the latter days, according to Ezekiel 38–39. This is a sign of the times that indicates we are likely near the beginning of the tribulation.

FORESHADOWS OF EZEKIEL'S PROPHECY

Ahmadinejad believes that the Mahdi will come some day very soon and that all the world will convert to Islam or die. The Bible predicts that Iran will join the ill-fated Gog and Magog coalition that will come against Israel in the end times and suffer a crushing defeat (Ezekiel 38–39). What we see in today's headlines bears remarkable resemblance to the coalition and conditions predicted in Ezekiel's ancient prophecy. Let me show you three such points of correspondence.

First, Ezekiel 37 predicts that the Jewish people will be regathered to their ancient homeland in the latter years. Ezekiel 38 presupposes that, at the time of the events it describes, the Jewish people are back in their land. Obviously, in order for the Jewish people in Israel to be attacked by the Gog coalition, they have to be living in their land. The regathering of the Jewish people back to their homeland began in the late 1800s and took a giant step on Friday, May 14, 1948, with the rebirth of the nation of Israel. After more than 1,900 years of exile, a huge contingent of the world's Jewish population was reunited in the Holy Land. As the regathering has continued, for the first time since AD 135, there are now more Jews in Israel than in any other place in the world.

Second, Ezekiel 38 prophesies that at some point in the last days, Israel will be living in great peace and enjoying abundant prosperity. Right now, with the chronic violence from the Palestinians and Hezbollah and the construction of the security fence in Israel, this seems like a dream. However, one of the main political and diplomatic issues in the world today is a Middle East peace plan. We hear about it weekly, if not daily. European and U.S. diplomats continue to explore some way to bring peace to Israel and her neighbors. Some form of a peace treaty must be hammered out before there can be any modicum of tranquillity in the Middle East. This is exactly what the Bible predicts in Ezekiel 38:8, 11:

> After many days you will be summoned; in the latter years
> you will come into the land that is restored from the sword,
> whose inhabitants have been gathered from many nations
> to the mountains of Israel which had been a continual
> waste; but its people were brought out from the nations,
> and they are living securely, all of them.... And you will

say, "I will go up against the land of unwalled villages. I will go against those who are at rest, that live securely, all of them living without walls and having no bars or gates."

This ancient prediction by Ezekiel appears to be on the horizon in the form of a Middle East peace plan that will be brokered by the West.

Third, Ezekiel 38 predicts that while Israel is living under this peace plan, a group of nations that includes Russia, Iran, Turkey, Libya, Sudan, and nations of central Asia will unleash an all-out attack aimed at wiping Israel off the face of the earth and taking her spoil. This is not too difficult to imagine today. Iran is contemplating application for membership in the Collective Security Treaty Organization (CTSO), which is a military alliance of Russia and other central Asian nations that came together after the fall of the Soviet Union. The current members are Russia, Kazakhstan, Kyrgyzstan, Uzbekistan, Armenia, Tajikistan, Azerbaijan, Georgia, and Belarus. All of these nations are within the geographical scope of ancient Rosh and Magog, which are two of the places listed in Ezekiel 38:1–7. Iran is already an observer in the organization but may soon be a full-fledged member. This is another step toward the formation of the Gog and Magog coalition.[3]

Israel continues to be a thorn in the side of these nations, all of whom are Muslim, except Russia. The hatred for Israel festers and grows each day. We don't know what twists and turns may occur in the days ahead, but when Israel finally is able to let down her guard after the peace treaty is put in place, these nations will carry out an evil sneak attack in an effort to "be like a cloud covering the land" (Ezekiel 38:9) and drive the Jews into the sea.

When these nations invade Israel, God will supernaturally intervene to deliver the Jewish people (Ezekiel 38:18–39:6). After this invasion the world will have to endure a few more years of the tribulation, but Jesus will end the time of trouble when He returns to planet earth as King of kings and Lord of lords. An awestruck world will see this glorious scene:

> And I saw heaven opened, and behold, a white horse, and He who sat on it is called Faithful and True, and in righteousness He judges and wages war. His eyes are a flame of fire, and on His head are many diadems; and He has a name written on Him which no one knows except Himself. He is clothed with a robe dipped in blood, and His name is called The Word of God. And the armies which are in heaven, clothed in fine linen, white and clean, were following Him on white horses. From His mouth comes a sharp sword, so that with it He may strike down the nations, and He will rule them with a rod of iron; and He treads the wine press of the fierce wrath of God, the Almighty. And on His robe and on His thigh He has a name written, "KING OF KINGS, AND LORD OF LORDS."
>
> Then I saw an angel standing in the sun, and he cried out with a loud voice, saying to all the birds which fly in midheaven, "Come, assemble for the great supper of God, so that you may eat the flesh of kings and the flesh of com-

manders and the flesh of mighty men and the flesh of
horses and of those who sit on them and the flesh of all
men, both free men and slaves, and small and great."

And I saw the beast and the kings of the earth and
their armies assembled to make war against Him who sat
on the horse and against His army. And the beast was
seized, and with him the false prophet who performed the
signs in his presence, by which he deceived those who had
received the mark of the beast and those who worshiped
his image; these two were thrown alive into the lake of fire
which burns with brimstone. And the rest were killed with
the sword which came from the mouth of Him who sat
on the horse, and all the birds were filled with their flesh.
(Revelation 19:11–21)

This is the *Apocalypse of Jesus Christ.* He is coming back as
Judge of all the earth. He will not be the second in command to
anyone, including the Mahdi.

THE FINAL INVITATION

When Jesus comes, every person will face Him as either Judge or
Savior. These are the only two choices. No one is exempt.

How about you? How will you face Him?

Jesus is the only way to God. Jesus Himself said so: "I am the
way, and the truth, and the life; no one comes to the Father but
through Me" (John 14:6). Jesus presented Himself as the narrow

gate that leads to life (Matthew 7:13) and as the only solid rock to build one's life upon (Matthew 7:24–25). I recognize that in our increasingly pluralistic society this kind of exclusive statement is difficult and even offensive to many people. But again, we can know that Jesus's words are true by remembering that He fulfilled hundreds of Old Testament prophecies and also predicted the future Himself with 100 percent accuracy. His deity is unquestionable. His works and words confirm it. Jesus is God in human flesh. Why not believe God's Word and accept God's Son as your personal Savior from sin? God has moved heaven and earth to make it plain. His record stands.

I think it's beautiful that the Apocalypse of Jesus ends with an open invitation. The last verses of the last book of the Bible end with a call to receive God's free gift of eternal life: "The Spirit and the bride say, 'Come.' And let the one who hears say, 'Come.' And let the one who is thirsty come; let the one who wishes take the water of life without cost" (Revelation 22:17). God offers the water of life free of charge to any thirsty soul who will simply take it.

Why not take your first drink of God's grace right now? If you do, you will never thirst again.

SOME QUESTIONS
YOU MIGHT BE ASKING

QUESTION 1: DOES THE BIBLE PREDICT A NUCLEAR WAR IN THE END TIMES?

Ever since the dawn of the nuclear age in the 1940s—with man's ability to blow up this planet—people have wondered if the world will end in a nuclear nightmare. According to a *Time* magazine poll (October 26, 1998), 51 percent of Americans believe that a man-made disaster will wipe out civilization during the next century.

The tense nuclear standoff between the United States and the Soviet Union was averted by the fear of what became known as Mutual Assured Destruction (MAD). However, the fear of a nuclear nightmare has returned with a vengeance, due to the recent proliferation of nuclear weapons. Nations such as Pakistan, North Korea, India, and China have nuclear weapons, and it seems only a matter of time until rogue states like Iran and fanatical terrorist organizations have access to the bomb.

This had led many people to wonder if the Bible has anything to say about nuclear explosions. Several passages of Scripture have been used to support the idea that the world will be destroyed by this means:

> Then it will be that he who flees the report of disaster will
>   fall into the pit,
> And he who climbs out of the pit will be caught in the
>   snare;
> For the windows above are opened, and the foundations
>   of the earth shake.
> The earth is broken asunder,
> The earth is split through,
> The earth is shaken violently.
> The earth reels to and fro like a drunkard
> And it totters like a shack,
> For its transgression is heavy upon it,
> And it will fall, never to rise again. (Isaiah 24:18–20)

> Now this will be the plague with which the LORD will
> strike all the peoples who have gone to war against Jeru-
> salem; their flesh will rot while they stand on their feet, and
> their eyes will rot in their sockets, and their tongue will rot
> in their mouth. (Zechariah 14:12)

> But by His word the present heavens and earth are being
> reserved for fire, kept for the day of judgment and destruc-

tion of ungodly men.... But the day of the Lord will come like a thief, in which the heavens will pass away with a roar and the elements will be destroyed with intense heat, and the earth and its works will be burned up. Since all these things are to be destroyed in this way, what sort of people ought you to be in holy conduct and godliness, looking for and hastening the coming of the day of God, because of which the heavens will be destroyed by burning, and the elements will melt with intense heat! But according to His promise we are looking for new heavens and a new earth, in which righteousness dwells. Therefore, beloved, since you look for these things, be diligent to be found by Him in peace, spotless and blameless. (2 Peter 3:7, 10–14)

The first sounded, and there came hail and fire, mixed with blood, and they were thrown to the earth; and a third of the earth was burned up, and a third of the trees were burned up, and all the green grass was burned up.

The second angel sounded, and something like a great mountain burning with fire was thrown into the sea; and a third of the sea became blood, and a third of the creatures which were in the sea and had life, died; and a third of the ships were destroyed.

The third angel sounded, and a great star fell from

heaven, burning like a torch, and it fell on a third of the rivers and on the springs of waters. The name of the star is called Wormwood; and a third of the waters became wormwood, and many men died from the waters, because they were made bitter.

The fourth angel sounded, and a third of the sun and a third of the moon and a third of the stars were struck, so that a third of them would be darkened and the day would not shine for a third of it, and the night in the same way. (Revelation 8:7–12)

I don't believe the Bible tells us clearly whether nuclear weapons will be used in the future on this earth. Many of the passages above seem to refer to divine judgment directly from the hand of God, rather than a nuclear explosion created by man. Nevertheless, however one interprets those passages, the Bible is clear that this world will not be destroyed by people. Genesis 1:1 tells us that God created the heavens and the earth, and we read in 2 Peter 3:5–7 that God will someday destroy the present heaven and earth with fire: "By the word of God the heavens existed long ago and the earth was formed out of water and by water, through which the world at that time was destroyed, being flooded with water. But by His word the present heavens and earth are being reserved for fire, kept for the day of judgment and destruction of ungodly men."

This passage makes clear that it is God Himself who will

"push the button" to destroy this world, not some Middle Eastern madman. The Bible begins with the words "In the beginning God..." It could end with the words "In the end God..." The God who created this world is in total control of His creation. Jesus is the alpha and the omega. He started it all, and He will end it all. There's not a maverick molecule in this vast universe. No man will ever destroy this earth. God has reserved that right for Himself.

And then after He has taken it all apart, the Lord will put it all back together again in a new heaven and new earth.

> Then I saw a new heaven and a new earth; for the first heaven and the first earth passed away, and there is no longer any sea. And I saw the holy city, new Jerusalem, coming down out of heaven from God, made ready as a bride adorned for her husband. And I heard a loud voice from the throne, saying, "Behold, the tabernacle of God is among men, and He will dwell among them, and they shall be His people, and God Himself will be among them, and He will wipe away every tear from their eyes; and there will no longer be any death; there will no longer be any mourning, or crying, or pain; the first things have passed away." (Revelation 21:1–4)

What comfort God provides His people in these turbulent times.

QUESTION 2: WHAT ABOUT NORTH KOREA? DON'T THEY ALREADY HAVE THE BOMB? AND ISN'T THEIR LEADER, KIM JONG IL, A LITTLE OFF CENTER? WHY IS AHMADINEJAD MORE DANGEROUS THAN THIS ECCENTRIC LEADER OF NORTH KOREA? WHY IS AHMADINEJAD THE WORLD'S MOST DANGEROUS MAN?

There's no doubt that Kim Jong Il is an international pariah. He's the brutal, autocratic leader of the world's most isolated nation—an Orwellian nation that now has the bomb and could pass nuclear weapons to nuclear wannabes like Iran or Syria. As the leader of a rogue state, he has defiantly taunted the world with his nuclear weapons. We know that he's short, pudgy, paranoid, reclusive, wears throwback Mao suits and platform shoes, and has a bad hairdo. His father was Kim Il Song, who ruled North Korea from 1945 to 1994. Kim Il Song was known as the "Great Leader" and was portrayed to the North Korean people as a divine emperor and god. Kim Jong Il, known as the Dear Leader, claims to be the Son of God. According to many sources, Kim Jong Il and his father are made out to be like God and Jesus Christ.

How could Ahmadinejad be more dangerous than Kim Jong Il?

The answer is found in Ahmadinejad's apocalyptic view of the end times. Kim Jong Il is a secular atheist. For him, when life is over, it's over. A man like that has a strong sense of self-preservation. Kim Jong Il lives a pampered life, eating the richest, most expensive foods while many of his people starve. But his atheistic belief system motivates him to live for self and to live as long as he can.

Ahmadinejad, on the other hand, believes that he can usher in the utopian society by paving the way for the Mahdi, the Islamic messiah figure. By faithfully fulfilling this mission, he believes that he can secure abundant rewards for himself in the coming new world order.

QUESTION 3: Are conservative Christians, who are waiting for their Messiah, just as dangerous as Ahmadinejad and Shiites, who claim that their Messiah is coming back?

In light of all that's happening in our world today, more and more people are asking this question. Many seem to believe that evangelical believers—who preach the Rapture of all living believers to heaven, a time of future tribulation for the earth, a future for the nation of Israel, and a personal return of Jesus back to earth—could actually be bringing these events to pass in a form of self-fulfilling prophecy.

On September 12, 2006, the ABC program *The View* broadcast a discussion about the 9/11 attacks on America. During the dialogue, cohost Rosie O'Donnell said, "Radical Christianity is just as threatening as radical Islam in a country like America, where we have a separation of church and state. We're a democracy here."

While Rosie is certainly no representative of mainstream thought, her startling statement does underline an uneasiness, or even fear, that some people have with any group of people who hold to a conservative, fundamentalist interpretation of their religious tenets.

For example, on March 22, 2007, New Jersey's Burlington Township High School held a hostage drill in the form of a mock terrorist attack. But in the emergency simulation, the attackers were not Islamic radicals. They were members of a right-wing, fundamentalist Christian group called the New Crusaders, who were upset that the daughter of one of the attackers was expelled for praying before class.[1] Of course, it's not inconceivable that some unhinged person could use the name of Christ to justify such actions, but it appears much more likely in today's world that the source of terror will come from Islamic radicals. However, in our modern culture of non-offense, Christians are a much softer target than radical Muslims.

This one incident serves to illustrate the moral equivalency that some people make between conservative Christians and radical Islam. But the proof for such equivalency is simply absent. First of all, do people really believe that conservative Christians have enough power to bring these events to pass? That they are actually powerful enough to set the world stage for their view of Armageddon?

Second, bear in mind the numerous sharp distinctions between conservative Christians and radical Muslims:

- Conservative Christians do not preach the genocide of a particular race of people. Radical Muslims do.
- Conservative Christians do not call for homicide bombers to slaughter innocent people. Radical Muslims do.

- Conservative Christians do not believe that they are to work for worldwide bloodshed, chaos, and war to bring back their Messiah. Radical Shiite Muslims do.
- Conservative Christians do not believe they can hasten the coming of Jesus. Radical Shiite Muslims do believe they can hasten the return of the Mahdi.
- Conservative Christians do not condone mutilation and maiming as punishment for criminal offenses. Radical Muslims do.
- Conservative Christians love Muslims, pray for them, support missionaries to Muslim lands, and desire the salvation of Muslim people. Radical Muslims call for jihad against the infidels.

But isn't it true that many conservative Christians are pro-Israel? Yes. Belief in the Bible and the promises of God to Abraham in Genesis 12:1–3 guide their actions and lead them to support the nation of Israel. The land of Israel is the only piece of real estate on earth that God specifically promised to a certain people. God promised blessing on those who would bless Abraham's descendants through Isaac and Jacob. Belief always issues forth in actions that are consistent with that belief—or so it should. But this does not make conservative Christians dangerous or radical. It simply means that they try to act consistently with their belief in what the Bible teaches. It also doesn't mean that they blindly condone everything Israel does. Christian Zionism is simply the belief that the Jewish people have the right to a national existence in their ancient homeland, as promised in the Bible. This is hardly radical.

QUESTION 4: COULD AHMADINEJAD BE THE BIBLICAL ANTICHRIST?

The last twenty years have brought some amazing developments into our world. People seem to have a sense that we may be getting near "closing time." As a result of this prophetic anticipation, many people today wonder if the Antichrist is alive right now somewhere on earth. Consider these statistics:[2]

- 49 percent of Americans believe there will be an Antichrist.
- 19 percent believe that the Antichrist is on earth now.
- 18 percent expect the end times to come within their lifetime.

Back in 1991, many people seriously wondered if Saddam Hussein could be the Antichrist. After all, the entire world was gathered in the Middle East against him. While that notion has disappeared, in light of Saddam's capture and execution, no one doubts that Saddam was a sinister, sly survivor who led the world to the brink of a serious crisis.

Clearly, Saddam was not the Antichrist. But could some other current, menacing world leader, such as Mahmoud Ahmadinejad, be the Antichrist predicted in the Bible. Many today are proposing the idea that the Antichrist may be a great Muslim leader who will bring the world together under the banner of Islam. Could

Ahmadinejad be that one? I believe we can say for certain that he is not.

My reasons are twofold. First, according to Daniel 9:26, the Antichrist will rise from the reunited Roman Empire, probably some nation in Western Europe. While parts of Asia and North Africa were part of the territory within the ancient Roman Empire, modern Iran (ancient Persia) was never part of the historical Roman Empire. Daniel 9:26 says specifically that the Antichrist will come from the same people who destroyed the Jewish temple in AD 70. Of course, this refers to the Romans. I don't believe this means that the Antichrist will necessarily be Italian, but it does seem to imply that he will rise from the core of the ancient Roman Empire, which is what we know today as Europe.

Second, the Bible says that the Antichrist will not be unveiled by God until the beginning of the tribulation period, which will be after the Rapture. As I often say, "If you ever do figure out who the Antichrist is, I've got bad news for you, you've been left behind." So I believe it is futile and speculative for us to even try to figure out the Antichrist's identity before the Rapture. The Bible is clear: we are to be looking for Christ, not the Antichrist.

However, having said that, vicious, cruel, arrogant dictators like Saddam and Ahmadinejad do strikingly foreshadow what the Antichrist will be like. Menacing madmen like Ahmadinejad do give us a small window into the Antichrist's character. History is littered with the lives of despotic dictators who prefigure what the final great man of sin will be like. These antichrists (plural with a little *a*) serve as types or examples of what *the* Antichrist (singular with a capital *A*) will be like.

First and Second John are the only two books in the New Testament that use the Greek word *antichristos* (1 John 2:18, 22; 2 John 7). These letters make a clear distinction between antichrists (plural) and *the* Antichrist (singular). With this in mind, as we look at history, who are some of history's little antichrists who picture what the Antichrist will be like?

- Nimrod (Genesis 10:8–11; 11:1–9)
- Alexander the Great (Daniel 8:5–8)
- Antiochus Epiphanes (Daniel 8:9–26)
- Nero Caesar
- Napoleon Bonaparte
- Adolf Hitler
- Joseph Stalin
- Saddam Hussein

Mike Wallace's *60 Minutes* interview with Ahmadinejad shows how these evil, nefarious leaders can, like the coming Antichrist, mask their true character under a veneer of smiles, personal charm, and charisma. Ahmadinejad was calm, incessantly smiling, well spoken, and measured. While Ahmadinejad clearly is not the Antichrist, he is another in the long line of antichrist-like figures who point toward what the final Antichrist will be like.

GLOSSARY OF TEN KEY TERMS

Allah—The name for God in the Islamic religion.

apocalypse—From the Greek word *apokalupsis,* it means to uncover or unveil something, or take the lid off.

ayatollah—Literally means "sign of God." It's the highest rank in the hierarchy of clerics in Shiite Islam.

Hojjatieh—A cultic Shiite group founded in Iran in 1953. They were originally founded to eradicate the Baha'i faith. The society focuses on the Twelfth or Hidden Imam and actively promotes the necessary conditions for his reappearance.

imam—In Sunni Islam, an imam is any person who leads prayer or delivers the sermon when Muslims gather on Fridays. For Shiites, the imam is a male descendant of Muhammad through Ali and Fatima.

Islam—Literally means "submission."

Koran or Qur'an—Literally means "recitation." It's the Muslim holy book, containing revelations given to Muhammad.

Mahdi—Islam's messiah figure, who will return in the last days to usher in a utopian era of peace, prosperity, and justice.

mullah—From the Arabic word *mawla*—"master," "lord," or "teacher"—it refers to any man with religious education. For Shiites, mullahs are the primary interpreters of Islamic law.

Muslim—Literally means "one who submits," a follower of the Islamic faith.

APPENDIX A

TRANSCRIPT OF A SPEECH BY AHMADINEJAD AT THE
"WORLD WITHOUT ZIONISM" CONFERENCE IN TEHRAN

Ahmadinejad gave the keynote speech on October 26, 2005, at the
gathering of four thousand students, organized by the Association
of Islamic Students Societies.[1]

I am grateful to God for giving me the great pleasure of
speaking at this very important gathering. I thank God for
seeing the pious faces of you, the valiant, aware, God-fearing,
and selfless children of the revolution, who understand with
vigilance and intelligence the most important issues of our
times and are active with great zest and in a decisive way in
the most central issues of the Islamic world. I thank God
for the presence of you dear young people.

The real question is what is Zionism? No doubt there
have been many discussions in this conference on this issue
and you have made studies in this regard, and you may
know what I want to emphasize, but it is something worth
mentioning.

We must see what the real story of Palestine is. Is the
conflict in Palestine a war between some Jews on the one
side and Muslims and non-Jews on the other side? Is it a

war between the Jews and other faiths? Is it the war of one country with other countries? Is it the war of one country with the Arab world? Is the conflict only over the limited lands of Palestine? I think the answer to all these questions is negative.

The creation of the regime occupying Al-Qods [Jerusalem] was a heavy move by the globally dominant system and Global Arrogance against the Islamic world. There is a historic battle going on between the Oppressor World and the Islamic world and the roots of this conflict go back hundreds of years.

In this historic conflict, the fronts have shifted many times. There were times when the Muslims had the upper hand and were active and forward-moving, while the Oppressor World was on retreat.

Unfortunately, in the past three hundred years, the Islamic world has been on retreat in the face of the Oppressor World.

I do not intend to go to the roots of the issue, and I concentrate on a historical review of the events. In the past one hundred years, the last trenches of the Islamic world fell and the Oppressor World created the regime occupying Al-Qods as the bridgehead for its domination of the Islamic world. Bridgehead is a military term in warfare. When two divisions or armies are fighting each other, if one side advances and breaks through the front and captures a piece of enemy territory and builds up fortifications and strengthens its hold to make it a base for further territorial expansion, then we call this a bridgehead.

The occupying state [Israel] is the bridgehead of the Oppressor World in the heart of the Islamic world. They have built a base to expand their domination to the entire Islamic world. There is no other raison d'être for this entity without this objective.

The battle that is going on in Palestine today, therefore, is the frontline of the conflict between the Islamic world and the Oppressor World. It is a battle of destiny that will determine the fate of hundreds of years of conflict in Palestine.

Today, the Palestinian nation is fighting the Oppressor World on behalf of the Islamic *umma* [nation]. Thank God, from the day the Palestinian nation moved toward an Islamic struggle with Islamic objectives and an Islamic environment and made Islam the dominating force in its behavior and orientation, we have been witnessing the progress and successes of the Palestinian nation every day.

I must say that you have chosen a very valuable title for your gathering ["World Without Zionism"]. Many are sowing the seeds of defeat and despair in this all-out war between the Islamic world and the Infidel Front, hoping to dishearten the Islamic world.

Such people are using words like "it's not possible." They say how could we have a world without America and Zionism? But you know well that this slogan and goal can be achieved and can definitely be realized.

If we take a look back, we had in our country a regime that was very violent, anti-popular, dependent on foreigners, and armed to its teeth. Members of SAVAK [the Shah's secret police] controlled every move and a terrible reign of terror existed.

But when the dear imam [Ruhollah Khomeini] said this regime must be destroyed, and we want a world without a client state, many of those who claim to be political gurus and other things said it's not possible. The day when the imam started his move, all the powers of the world supported that corrupt regime. Even after the massacre of Black Friday, the West and the East and regional powers all supported the regime. But our nation fought and now for twenty-seven years we have a government that is independent of America. The imam said the domination of the East and the West must be destroyed, but weak-minded persons, who only see the little world around them, didn't believe him....

Our dear imam ordered that the occupying regime in Al-Qods be wiped off the face of the earth. This was a very wise statement. The issue of Palestine is not one on which we could make a piecemeal compromise.... This would mean our defeat. Anyone who would recognize this state [Israel] has put his signature under the defeat of the Islamic world.

In his struggle against the World Arrogance, our dear imam targeted the central and command base of the enemy, namely the occupying regime in Al-Qods. I have no doubt that the new wave that has started in dear Palestine and which we witness today all over the Islamic world will soon wipe this scourge of shame from the Islamic world. This can be done.

We have to watch out for conspiracies. For more than fifty years, the World Arrogance has tried to give recognition to the existence of this fake regime [Israel] and they have made many efforts to first stabilize it and then take further steps.

Some twenty-seven or twenty-eight years ago, they took an important step in this regard and, unfortunately, one of the frontline countries made this mistake, and we hope that country [Egypt] will rectify its mistake.

Recently, a new conspiracy has been plotted and is underway. They have been forced to evacuate a corner of Palestine and this was imposed on them by the Palestinian nation. But they want to sell this as the final victory and use the evacuation of Gaza and the creation of a Palestinian state as an excuse to end the Palestinian cause and goal.

Today they are making an evil and deceptive effort to turn the struggle into an internal conflict of the Islamic world. They want to create conflict among Palestinian groups inside Palestine by making them greedy for political positions or high office, so that these groups abandon the decisive issue of Palestine and turn on each other.

With the excuse of having cleared the Gaza Strip to

show their good will, they want a group of Muslim nations to recognize this corrupt regime, and I am very hopeful and pray to God that the Palestinian nation and the dear Palestinian groups will be cautious of such sedition.

Today the unity of the front in Palestine on its goals is a pressing necessity. The issue of Palestine is by no means finished. The issue of Palestine will only be resolved when all of Palestine comes under Palestinian rule, when all the refugees return to their homes, and when a popular government chosen by this nation takes the affairs in its hands. Of course, those who have come to this land from far away to plunder this land have no right to participate in the decision-making process for this nation.

I am hopeful that just as the Palestinian nation continued its struggle for the past ten years, it will continue to maintain its awareness and vigilance. This phase is going to be short-lived. If we put it behind us successfully, God willing, it will pave the way for the annihilation of the Zionist regime and it will be a downhill route.

I warn all the leaders in the Islamic world to beware of this conspiracy. If any of them takes a step towards the recognition of this regime [Israel], then he will burn in the fire of the Islamic *umma* [nation] and will have eternal shame stamped on his forehead, regardless of whether he did this under pressure by the dominant powers or lack of understanding or naiveté or selfishness or worldly incentives.

The issue of Palestine is the issue of the Islamic world. Those who are closeted behind closed doors cannot make decisions on this issue and the Islamic nation does not allow this historical enemy to exist at the heart of the Islamic world.

APPENDIX B

AHMADINEJAD'S FIRST BLOG ENTRY ON AUGUST 8, 2006

One of the more interesting endeavors Ahmadinejad has undertaken to propagate his mystical views is his Web site and blog (www.ahmadinejad.ir). I thought you might find his initial blog enlightening.

> In the Name of God, the Most Merciful, the Most Compassionate.
>
> Oh Almighty God, please, we beg you to send us our Guardian—who You have promised us—soon and appoint us as His close companions.
>
> During the era that nobility was a prestige and living in a city was perfection, I was born in a poor family in a remote village of Garmsar—approximately 90 kilometer east of Tehran. I was born fifteen years after Iran was invaded by foreign forces—in August of 1940—and the time that another puppet, named Mohammad Reza—the son of Reza Mirpange—was set as a monarch in Iran. Since the extinct shah—Mohammad Reza—was supposed to take and enter Iran into western civilization slavishly, so many schemes were implemented that Iran becomes another market for the western ceremonial goods without any progress in the

scientific field. Our Islamic culture would not allow such an infestation, and this was an impediment in front of shah and his foreign masters' way. Thus, they decided to make this noble and tenacious culture weak gradually that Iran be attached strongly to the west as far as its economy, politics, and culture was concern. After the implementation of this policy and the unreal and outward of upswing, the villagers began to rush to the cities. Upon the enforcement of the land reform, the status of the villages became worst than the past and villagers for earning some breadcrumbs, they were deceived by the dazzling look and the misleading features of the cities and became suburban and lived in ghettos.

My family was also suffered in the village as others. After my birth—the fourth one in the family—my family was under more pressures. My father had finished 6 grade of elementary school. He was a hard-bitten toiler black-smith, a pious man who regularly participated in different religious programs. Even though never the dazzling look of the world was appealing to him, but the pressure of the life caused that he decided to migrate to Tehran when I was one year old. We chose to live in south central part of Tehran where is called Pamenar.

■ ■ ■

My father used to buy newspaper all the time. I remember one day, when I was in first grade, by looking through a newspaper—with the help of the adults in our house—I read the news of the capitulation passage by the shah's so called "parliament." Even though I did not understand the meaning of that issue at that time, but due to the protests and the objections of the religious schools of thoughts with the leadership of Imam Khomeini—Almighty God bless his soul—and the relentless reaction of the extinct shah, I realized that Mohammad Reza attempted to add another page to his vicious case history which was the humiliation and indignity of the Iranian people versus Americans. That was the year that the extinct shah slaughtered many followers of Imam Khomeini.

Imam Khomeini was released from prison. I never forget Imam Khomeini's speeches during those years which was very persuasive and appealing. You would hear the strong faith to Almighty God in his orations. He invited the people to pure Islam. His message was invitation to the belief of monotheism—Unity and Oneness of God—and also justice, elimination of oppression, injustice and sedition in the world. He was courageous and had a valiant heart. He spoke firmly and securely. His orations were simple and honest. The people accepted his guidance sincerely. Due to these characteristics, he was a beloved leader for every individuals—young or elderly. Of course he was a disgrace for shah's regime and his Americans masters. Notably, even among his enemies, he was respected with a special honor.

■ ■ ■

Eventually, the existence of Imam Khomeini was unbear-
able for the extinct shah and he could not tolerate him any
more. Since they knew if they kill him—as they did a great
number of his followers—the bloody uprising can not be
controlled. Consequently they decided to exile him in order
to separate the leader from his followers and to restrain the
revolution which was occurring. They send him into exile
overnight and his exile lasted 14 years.

While Imam Khomeini was in exile, I became more
familiar with his ideas, thoughts and philosophy through
his companions and disciples in different classes and meet-
ings. The more I became familiar with his thoughts and
philosophy, the more affection I had for that divine leader
and his separation and absence was intolerable for me.
Although the enemies of the Iranian Muslims separated
their leader from them, but always he was in people's hearts
and was more close to them than ever.

■ ■ ■

When I used to go to high school, shah celebrated the
2500 years of monarchy of Iran. Those years, poverty
among the oppressed people of Iran was escalated and dou-
bled. The imposition of the cost and the expenditure of

these festivals and ceremonies and also the crapulence of shah's debauched clan and their foreign companies, broke the people's back. All necessary materials and supplies of these illegitimate functions were brought to Iran from Europe by the exclusive and specific airplanes. Probably one can claim that the disgraceful festivals of the 2500 years of kingdom in Iran—which was arranged by the traitorous shah—were the most expensive festivals in the history of the civilized human.

Anyway, in this situation, my father's sledgehammer and anvil could not cover my family's necessary expenses. Thus, I had to start working in a shop—that made certain parts for cooling system of buildings—to make some money to cover a portion of my family's expenses and also my educational costs. Even though I was very playful those days, but was aware of my school & education. I was a distinguished student. From that time, I was interested and attached to teaching. I used to teach my friends and others in their houses. The last year of my high school, I prepared myself for university admission test-conquer. And later on that year, I took the test. Although I had nose bleeding during the test, but I became 132nd student among over 400 thousand participants. I was admitted for civil engineering major in one of the technical universities in Tehran. That was three years before the revolution. Even though the revolution was taking place and I was involved in certain activities against

the illegitimate regime of the monarch in Iran—the mercenary & puppet of U.S. & Britain—but I was aware of my
education and did not give it up.

■ ■ ■

In order to stop the university students from joining the
revolution, the traitorous shah and his clan tried to abolish
Islamic belief and revolutionary motives among students,
by propagating immorality, promiscuity, and perversion in
universities in Iran. Although a small number of students
fell into their traps, but in general, university converted to a
base for demonstration against shah's regime. The people's
faith and devotion to Islam was the main reason that they
became ready to face bloodthirsty shah with his brutal and
savage torture and encounter his death squad.

■ ■ ■

Imam Khomeini—after being in exile in Iraq and else-
where—came back to Iran. The manner in which Imam
Khomeini was warmly welcomed on his return after fifteen
years of exile by Iranian nation will always be remembered
in the records of history. Whole Iran poured out in the
streets to welcome Imam. The eyes of those watching Iran
from the outside world were dazzled to see this great event

and they were helpless to understand and come up with an explanation for what they saw.

The Islamic Revolution of the nation of Iran achieved victory after several years of severe hardships, brave perseverance and sacrifices of thousands of martyrs to the unbelievable astonishment of political analysts of East and West and right in front of the watchful eyes of Intelligence apparatuses of the great World powers at that time. Our Revolution was unique in its own kind. The whole Iranian nation with empty hands and only relying on the divine weapon of faith and under the leadership of an 80 years old man, was able to give a crushing defeat to the mercenary of USA, the Shah (King) of Iran and disclose the real disgraceful face of his powerful supporters to the countries of the region and the whole world.

■ ■ ■

Although, right at the beginning of the movement of Imam Khomeini, the type of Government Imam was seeking to establish was known to everybody, however, Imam repeatedly laid great emphasis that everyone's opinion should be taken into consideration (by holding a referendum) for the establishment of the type of new government in Iran. This he did so as to show right at the outset that it is with the wishes of the nation as well as in accordance with the principles of Islam, that an Islamic Government is established. Although, there was absolutely no need of a referendum, but Imam with his wise foresight, proved his point of view to everyone and left no place for those who wished to seek alternatives. This action of Imam and vehement participation and positive reply to the establishment of Islamic Republic by the Iranian nation, caused disappointment of some of the political groups that were affiliated to great world powers. These terrorist groups with the support and directions from arrogant powers, the leader of them being USA at that time, started massacring innocent people as well as the leading figures of the Islamic Revolution. They, like their supporting masters, thought that they can undermine and collapse the new government right in its beginning. But, the nation of Iran was not ready to give this precious and great Revolution from their hands so easily. They stood firmly and with great difficulties, remained loyal to Revolution and protected it at all costs. They were ultimately able to force these terrorist groups out of their own country. Although these terrorist groups are still under the protection and shameful support of Great Satan USA, however, the slap that these groups have received from the brave nation of Iran will never be forgotten by them.

The global arrogance had determined to defeat the Islamic Revolution of Iran at all costs. The reason was that they were afraid that this revolution will become a model and ideal path for other nations in the region and in the world. On the other they also wished to get back their lost prestige. Thus, they, in addition to supporting daily terrorist activities inside Iran, they also supported regime of Saddam to attack Iran and start the imposed war. The analysis of corrupt politicians at that time was that Iranian revolution was in its beginning and the government was not fully established and was not powerful enough to survive. The security apparatus of state, they thought, was not fully functional and was weak and didn't have enough weaponry and experience. And, on the other side was Saddam, whatever he wanted, they provided him, and they thought that he will win the war on Iran. Saddam, intoxicated with power and while receiving all the economic, military and intelligence support that USA and other Western countries provided him, proudly announced that he will capture Tehran within 3 days. The war that was imposed on Iran, continued for more than 8 years instead of 3 days and ultimately in the end, not even an inch of Iranian land reach the hands of Saddam and his supporters.

During these 8 years, Saddam fought with us and also with his own people. He bombarded our cities with chemical weapons provided by the Western powers and also Iraqi villages and towns. During the whole period of war, while Saddam was bombarding our cities, Islamic Republic of Iran, obeying the laws of Islam and humanitarian principles, never attacked cities and limited the war with the army of Iraq in the battlefield. It is sad, that even this humane

attitude of Islamic Republic didn't impress those who at
world stage watched the war at that time.

■ ■ ■

At the beginning of war, I was 25 years of age. My mother
and wife and all the mothers and wives of the Iranian
nation, whose youths and their wives participated in war
and defended their country, patiently trained and educated
the next generation, which is brave, resisting and faithful.
Today's brave and strong youths are the fruits of hardships
and untiring efforts of the days of past.

The sacred defense in the universities was related to
teaching human values. Side by side, the experience of life
and death during war made this life like a heaven on earth
and hereafter, such that what was said and heard about it
and carried out at that time, was truly godly.

Brotherhood, faithfulness, seriousness and loving hard
work, spirituality and worship, eagerness and happiness to
do good, sacrifice and bravery, all these values have proved
to us time and again that this world and hereafter are not
opposite to each other, rather they both are completely in
harmony with each other. At that time, martyrdom was the
only wish of our defending fighters.

In the year 1988, one year before the demise of Imam
Khomeini, may peace of God be upon him, the United
Nations Security Council passed the resolution to stop the

war and Imam unwillingly accepted it and announced that this acceptance on his part is like drinking poison. The war ended and in a situation when all the international organizations strived very hard to distort and hide the facts that Saddam was the aggressor and that the arrogant powers had fully supported him. For those who were not aware of the close working of these international organizations and arrogant powers of the world, this indifference to and distortion and hiding of the facts was a very shocking experience.

■ ■ ■

I will continue this topic later on as it took long in the beginning. From now onwards, I will try to make it shorter and simpler.

With hope in God, I intend to wholeheartedly complete my talk in future with allotted fifteen minutes.

APPENDIX C

Official Iranian Eschatology Outlined in the
Public Broadcasting Program in Iran

The following are excerpts from the transcripts of the *World Toward
Illumination* program from the Islamic Republic of Iran Broadcasting Web site (http://english.irib.ir/iran/Leader/Illumination
.htm).

The English translation below is from MEMRI (*Middle East
Media Research Institute,* no. 1436, January 25, 2007).

This provides an excellent summary and overview of Shiite
eschatology and shines the light squarely on Ahmadinejad and his
vision for the world. This is what he expects to happen. This is
what he is working feverishly to bring to fruition.

1: Miracles of the Messiah Will Soon Be Here

> …Where is man moving to? What will happen in his
> future? What fate will today's nations and civilizations
> have in the future? Will they destroy one another? Will a
> power, nation or civilization prevail? And finally to what
> direction will the speed of technology and modernity take
> man?…

In the current era new interpretations of happiness
and prosperity for man have been brought up. In these
interpretations there is talk about welfare and worldly tranquility. Some believe that science and material progress
automatically bring about prosperity, and man can attain
sublimity on earth.... But the world's reality shows that
man more than any other time is searching for prosperity
and tranquility. The daily increasing production of destructive weapons, domineering tendencies, racist wars, genocide
and instability of world markets, all threaten the world's
security and tranquility. Now western rulers under the slogan of liberal democracy are tyrannically and oppressively
looting the capital of oppressed nations. The weakness of
the family foundation, crime, violence, narcotics, human
trafficking, anxiety and depression have faced the world's
future with serious danger....

We invite you to tune in to our next programs to see
how the future will turn out to be. And we invite you to
listen to an inspiring poem.

Be joyous my heart, miracles of the Messiah will soon
  be here
The scent of breaths of the One we know comes from
  near
Grieve not of sorrow and melancholy, as assured I
  was...last night
That a Savior will come, it's clear.

3: How Beautiful and Auspicious Will Be the Day when the World Is Cleansed of Deceit

How beautiful and auspicious will be the day when the world is cleansed of deceit and mischief and the government of justice is established throughout the world.

On that day the perfume of life will begin to circulate within humans and the aroma of narcissus, irises and chrysanthemums will fill their soul. Undoubtedly such a day is nigh.

Seeking pure water so thirsty am I,

Moonlight surely appeals to my eye

Oh bright dawn I desire you as I sigh

The luminous sun I seek or I die.

6: We Must Get Ready to Search for the Liberal Democratic Civilization in History Museums

The West due to a lack of spirituality and morality is not able to respond to man's needs. Lack of attention to man's sublime needs in these societies has created social and cultural crises. Thus this civilization like those of many other Western theoreticians is just an unreal theory. It seems that in the same way that the Father of the Islamic Revolution, Imam Khomeini predicted the fall of communism we must get ready to search for the liberal democratic civilization in history museums.

12: Everything Will Be New and Fresh Like Spring

Undoubtedly, history will not end with the memory of man's failures; man's ultimate fate is not weakness and inability; and the sun will undoubtedly not spare its vital rays from anyone. Many Iranian poets have spoken of the rise of the sun at dawn and consider man to be worthy of living in a bright and beautiful world full of the aroma of spirituality, where there is justice and equality....

Contrary to the views of western theoreticians, who usually depict an ambiguous and dark future for mankind, Muslim experts believe human history, despite its many ups and downs, has a very auspicious fate, and with the appearance of the Imam of the Age, Hazrat Mahdi (may God hasten his reappearance), finally the world matters will gain order. Muslims believe hopes for the realization of such a happy ending for the world, are called "Awaiting Redemption," and means waiting for man's problems to be solved by the Savior at the end of time. This awaiting influences many, and inspires them with activity and enthusiasm in confronting darkness and oppression for changing the existing situation....

When that Promised Person who is the direct descendant of the Prophet rises up, the sun of justice and freedom will shine on the hearts and he with his kind hands will extend friendship throughout the world. His face will be attractive and his look charismatic. He is humble before

God's greatness. He is a manifestation of God's glory and beauty. Imam Mahdi is the perfect human being. His behavior is praiseworthy and his manners immaculate. He is the embodiment of justice. His torch of guidance is for all mankind....

In short, when he reappears, peace, justice and security will overcome oppression and deceit and one global government, the most perfect ever, will be established. He will make the earth prosper in a way in which no ruins will remain. Man's maturity will reach its height, full equality will be established among the people, and no one will be arrogant toward the other and will not try to dominate others. Finally, corruption, war and rebellion will no longer exist and everything will be new and fresh like spring.

13: PURE AND SINCERE PEOPLE MUST BE TRAINED TO HELP THE SAVIOR IN HIS IMPLEMENTATION OF GLOBAL JUSTICE

Sometimes incidents that occur in the world are like an insignificant but infectious pimple that suddenly explodes. Some theoreticians support this view and believe that nothing should stop this volcanic explosion and we should allow corruption to extend so much that the prevailing system would disintegrate. But the uprising of Imam Mahdi...is not like this. This uprising is like a fruit that must pass through stages till it is ready to be picked. Thus, if the

Savior has not yet appeared it is not because the world is not full of oppression, but because the time must come for the people to be wise enough and ready to accept justice. Pure and sincere people must be trained in order to help the Savior in his implementation of global justice…

MONDAY, NOVEMBER 20, 2006: THE SEAT OF THE MAHDI'S GLOBAL GOVERNMENT WILL BE THE CITY OF KUFA [IN IRAQ]

He will appear as a handsome young man, clad in neat clothes and exuding the fragrance of paradise. His face will glow with love and kindness for the human beings and because of this reason a famous hadith from the Prophet of Islam…has referred to him as *Inn-al-Mahdi Tavous ahl al-Jannah,* which means "Indeed the Mahdi will be like a Peacock among the People of Paradise." He has a radiant forehead, black piercing eyes and a broad chest. He very much resembles his ancestor Prophet Mohammad.… Heavenly light and justice accompany him. He will overcome enemies and oppressors with the help of God, and as per the promise of the Almighty the Mahdi will eradicate all corruption and injustice from the face of the earth and establish the global government of peace, justice and equity.

Imam Mahdi (may God hasten his reappearance) will appear all of a sudden on the world scene with a voice from the skies announcing his reappearance at the holy Ka'ba in

Mecca. The cloak and other special belongings of Prophet
Mohammad…will be with him. He is the essence of all
good and the mirror reflecting the characteristics of the
124,000 Prophets sent by God for the guidance of mankind since creation. He calls on all and says I am Baqiat-
Allah or the Repository of God on earth. The Prophet had
said: Mahdi will appear with a cloud moving above his
head. From the sky it will be announced that the hands of
the oppressors have been cut and the best of men from the
progeny of Mohammad has taken over the leadership.
Then the birds will lay abundant eggs and the fish will
exceedingly reproduce, the rivers will flow in all their glory
and the springs will gush forth from the earth, and the
fruits will be multiplied.

In our discussion of the world in the last days of the
earth we had said in our previous editions of this program
that no source has pointed to the exact date when the Savior will appear and only God knows about the exact timing
of the reappearance of Imam Mahdi…. The Prophet had
said: He will certainly appear and if only a day were to be
left to the end of the world God will make that day so long
for Mahdi to appear and rise. There are various versions of
the exact day of his reappearance. Some say it would be Friday and the date will be Ashura or the 10th of Moharram,
the heart-rending martyrdom anniversary of his illustrious
ancestor, Imam Husain…. Others say the date will be the
25th of the month of Zil-Qa'dah and may coincide with

the Spring Equinox or Nowrooz as the Iranians call [it]. A saying attributed to the Prophet's 6th infallible heir, Imam Ja'far Sadeq...says the Mahdi will appear on the Spring Equinox and God will make him defeat Dajjal the Impostor or the anti-Christ as the Christians say, who will be hanged near the dump of Kufa....

Then he will be joined by 313 of the most devoted believers, equivalent to the number of those that had accompanied the Prophet at the Battle of Badr, the first armed encounter imposed by the infidels on the Muslims. Imam Mahdi and steadfast devotees will gather in Mecca; the people of Mecca will be surprised at the presence of so many faithful. These enlightened individuals will pledge allegiance to the Mahdi....

After his appearance the Imam would remain in Mecca for some time, and then go to Medina. According to narrations, Sofyani, a descendant of the Prophet's archenemy Abu Sofyan, will seize Syria and attack Iraq and the Hejaz with the ferocity of a beast. The Sofyani will commit great crimes against humanity in Iraq, slaughtering people bearing the names of the infallible Imams, and his army will lay siege to the city of Kufa and to Holy Najaf. Of course, many incidents take place in this line and finally Imam Mahdi sends troops who kill the Sofyani in Beit ol-Moqaddas [i.e., Jerusalem], the Islamic holy city in Palestine that is currently under occupation of the Zionists. Soon a pious person from the progeny of Imam Hasan Mojtaba...meets with the Imam. He is a venerable God-fearing individual from Iran. Before the Imam's appearance he fights oppression and corruption and enters Iraq to lift the siege of Kufa and holy Najaf and to defeat the forces of Sofyani in Iraq. He then pledges allegiance to Imam Mahdi.

Another beautiful moment of the Savior's appearance is the coming down of Prophet Jesus…from heaven. Hazrat Mahdi receives him courteously and asks him to lead the prayers. But Jesus says you are more qualified for this than me. We read in the book Tazkarat ol-Olia, "the Mahdi will come with Jesus son of Mary accompanying him." This indicates that these two great men…complement each other. Imam Mahdi will be the leader while Prophet Jesus will act as his lieutenant in the struggle against oppression and [for the] establishment of justice in the world. Jesus had himself given the tidings of the coming of God's last messenger and will see Mohammad's ideals materialize in the time of the Mahdi. The seat of the Mahdi's global government will be the city of Kufa, where his headquarters will be the Sahla Mosque, presently outside the city that was the home of Prophet Idrees or Enoch long before the great deluge of the times of Prophet Noah. From here he will dominate the east and the west to fill the earth with justice.…

God will enliven the earth through the Mahdi after the corruption and vice wrought by the oppressors and sinner[s]. Thus his appearance will take place when morality and humanity have reached a dead end. The people's yearning for justice in the midst of all the oppression allows him to carry out his mission. In our time, many pray for his appearance and each day they renew their allegiance to him. "O God, make me one of his companions, show me his respected and bright visage, and hasten his reappearance.

Monday, November 27, 2006: After His Uprising from Mecca, All of Arabia Will Submit to Him, and Then Other Parts of the World as He Marches on Iraq

When the sun of freedom and justice shines, the sounds of a rider coming from afar will be heard. The winds obey him, and in his presence the turbulent seas and fiery storms will reach the shore of calmness. The appearance of the Savior will make the fragrance of eternal justice embellish the soul of the earth. The Mahdi…himself will say, my existence is the cause of security and peace for the world people.

There are various narrations on the global government of peace and justice of Imam Mahdi (may God hasten his reappearance and cleanse the Planet of all vestiges of sin and corruption). Narrations on the global government of justice, the universal government, the government of the deprived, the government of welfare and security, and each of these indicates one aspect of the Savior's government. The justice-spreading universal government encompasses all these. Prophet Mohammad…has been quoted as saying: I give you the good tidings of the Mahdi. He will rise in my *ummah* [i.e., the Muslim nation], while my *ummah* is entangled in differences and deviations. He will fill the earth that is immersed in oppression, with justice. And all those in heaven and earth will be content with him....

One of the first measures of Imam Mahdi…is fighting all centers of domination and power-mongering. In this way, Global Arrogance [i.e., the West, headed by America] and its minions puffed up by their economic and military might will try to create problems but they will not be able to change anything in their favor. The Mahdi considers his programs within the framework of conventional criteria, and says: Fear God and surrender to us and hand over the affairs to us. It is up to us to quench your thirst from the spring, as we are the one[s] who take you to its source.

The Mahdi's far-sightedness and firmness in the face of mischievous elements will strike awe. After his uprising from Mecca, all of Arabia will…submit to him and then other parts of the world as he marches upon Iraq and estab-lished his seat of global government in the city of Kufa. Then the Imam will send 10 thousand of his forces to the east and west to uproot the oppressors. At this time God will facilitate things for him and lands will come under his control one after the other. The Prophet's 5th infallible suc-cessor, Imam Mohammad Baqer…says: It is as if I see the Mahdi who has taken control of the east and the west, and all obey him.

Thus, as is clear, in the justice-seeking government the clouds give way to bright sunshine, as the Promised Savior spreads his radiance on the earth. God's infinite kindness will give refuge to mankind and the brightness of truth and justice will be seen in all dimensions of life.

MONDAY, DECEMBER 11, 2006: THE IDEA OF PLACING HUMANITY UNDER ONE RELIGION…IS A GIFT GIVEN BY ISLAM TO HUMANITY

Regarding the Islamic goal of the perfect and ideal state, it should be noted that the world desired by Islam is not a far-fetched idea like the utopia of the West in which the realities of today's society have no effect. Since the natural growth of man is toward sublimity, dedicated Muslims in each and every era strive to materialize the characteristics of the promised society to the best of their ability.… The Father of the Islamic Revolution, Imam Khomeini (may his soul rest in peace) used to emphasize this and would say: We, of course, cannot fill the world with justice now. If we could we certainly would. But since we cannot, he, the Savior must come. The world is full of oppression and if we can prevent oppression we will have carried out our part of the duty.…

With the reappearance of Imam Mahdi…conflicts, differences and discriminations that stem from lack of faith and atheism in the society will be eliminated. The shortcomings of religions and schools of thought will be clarified and Islam will prevail as the perfect pinnacle of faith. In other words, methods will become one and oneness will appear in people's beliefs. The Mahdi will materialize the call of the holy Qur'an, which throughout its text has urged mankind to unite and worship the One and the Only God without associating partners to him. The writer of the book *Imamate and Mahdaviyat* says: the idea of placing humanity under one religion irrespective of their color, gender, language, class and ethnicity is a gift given by Islam to humanity....

MONDAY, DECEMBER 25, 2006: THE UNJUST SYSTEM OF DISTRIBUTION AND DENIAL OF THE RIGHTS OF NATIONS WILL END WITH THE REAPPEARANCE OF IMAM MAHDI

In the weird system of today's powerful count[r]ies, moral and spiritual values have no place and are seen as undesirable liabilities that prevent these powers from reaching economic welfare and what they call true prosperity. However, the exploitation of the weak, the unjust system of distribution and denial of the rights of nations, will end with the reappearance of Imam Mahdi....

One of the characteristics of the global government of the Mahdi is the astounding growth of science and technology. There will be an explosion of science. As we said last week, knowledge is made of 27 letters and up to now whatever man has discovered is within the confines of only 2 letters. But when the Mahdi appears the other 25 letters of knowledge will be at the service of mankind, which is something not imaginable with the limited knowledge that we have today despite the seemingly great progress in science and technology. The Mahdi will correct man's scientific mistakes and bring up new and astonishing methods that had never occurred to man before.... The Mahdi will also regain the wealth and properties that have unrightfully been usurped by invaders and oppressors and distribute divine blessings among the people. Imam Baqer...says he will divide them with such equality that there will no longer be any poor person. In Islam's logic justice and good relations among people will lead to the flow of abundant divine blessings from the sky. Since people will have the best of qualities vital rains will pour down and all the earth will be filled with greenness and freshness. The Prophet had said in this regard: in my *ummah,* the Mahdi will rise and people will gain such welfare as never seen before. The sky will repeatedly rain and the earth will hide none of the things it can grow.

APPENDIX D

AHMADINEJAD'S OPEN LETTER TO PRESIDENT BUSH

The following translation from Farsi to English is from Reuters.

Mr. George Bush, president of the United States of America.

For some time now, I have been thinking, how one can justify the undeniable contradictions that exist in the international arena—which are being constantly debated, especially in political forums and amongst university students. Many questions remain unanswered. Those have prompted me to discuss some of the contradictions and questions, in the hopes that it might bring about an opportunity to redress them.

Can one be a follower of Jesus Christ (Peace Be Upon Him), the great Messenger of God, feel obliged to respect human rights, present liberalism as a civilization model, announce one's opposition to the proliferation of nuclear weapons and WMDs, make "War on Terror" his slogan, and finally, work towards the establishment of an unified international community—a community which Christ and the virtuous of the Earth will one day govern,

But at the same time,

Have countries attacked. The lives, reputations and

possessions of people destroyed and on the slight chance of
the presence of a few criminals in a village, city, or convoy
for example, the entire village, city or convoy set ablaze.

Or because of the possibility of the existence of WMDs
in one country, it is occupied, around 100,000 people
killed, its water sources, agriculture and industry destroyed,
close to 180,000 foreign troops put on the ground, sanc-
tity of private homes of citizens broken, and the country
pushed back perhaps 50 years. At what price? Hundreds of
billions of dollars spent from the treasury of one country
and certain other countries and tens of thousands of young
men and women—as occupation troops—put in harms
way, taken away from family and loved ones, their hands
stained with the blood of others, subjected to so much
psychological pressure that every day some commit suicide
and those returning home suffer depression, become sickly
and grapple with all sorts of ailments; while some are killed
and their bodies handed to their families.

On the pretext of the existence of WMDs, this great
tragedy came to engulf both the peoples of the occupied
and the occupying country. Later it was revealed that no
WMDs existed to begin with.

Of course, Saddam was a murderous dictator. But the
war was not waged to topple him, the announced goal of
the war was to find and destroy weapons of mass destruction. He was toppled along the way towards another goal;
nevertheless the people of the region are happy about it. I

point out that throughout the many years of the imposed war on Iran Saddam was supported by the West.

Mr. President,

You might know that I am a teacher. My students ask me how can these actions be reconciled with the values outlined at the beginning of this letter and duty to the tradition of Jesus Christ (Peace Be Upon Him), the Messenger of peace and forgiveness?

There are prisoners in Guantanamo Bay that have not been tried, have no legal representation, their families cannot see them and are obviously kept in a strange land outside their own country. There is no international monitoring of their conditions and fate. No one knows whether they are prisoners, POWs, accused or criminals.

European investigators have confirmed the existence of secret prisons in Europe too. I could not correlate the abduction of a person, and him or her being kept in secret prisons, with the provisions of any judicial system. For that matter, I fail to understand how such actions correspond to the values outlined in the beginning of this letter, i.e., the teachings of Jesus Christ (Peace Be Upon Him), human rights and liberal values.

Young people, university students, and ordinary people have many questions about the phenomenon of Israel. I am sure you are familiar with some of them.

Throughout history, many countries have been occupied, but I think the establishment of a new country with a new people, is a new phenomenon that is exclusive to our times.

Students are saying that 60 years ago such a country did not exist. They show old documents and globes and say try as we have, we have not been able to find a country named Israel.

I tell them to study the history of WWI and II. One of my students told me that during WWII, which more than tens of millions of people perished in, news about the war, was quickly disseminated by the warring parties. Each touted their victories and the most recent battlefront defeat of the other party. After the war they claimed that six million Jews had been killed. Six million people that were surely related to at least two million families. Again let us assume that these events are true. Does that logically translate into the establishment of the state of Israel in the Middle East or support for such a state? How can this phenomenon be rationalized or explained?

Mr. President,

I am sure you know how—and at what cost—Israel was established:

- Many thousands were killed in the process.
- Millions of indigenous people were made refugees.
- Hundreds of thousands of hectares of farmland, olive plantations, towns and villages were destroyed.

This tragedy is not exclusive to the time of establishment; unfortunately it has been ongoing for 60 years now.

A regime has been established which does not show mercy even to kids, destroys houses while the occupants are still in them, announces beforehand its list and plans to assassinate Palestinian figures, and keeps thousands of Palestinians in prison. Such a phenomenon is unique—or at the very least extremely rare—in recent memory.

Another big question asked by the people is "why is this regime being supported?"

Is support for this regime in line with the teachings of Jesus Christ (Peace Be Upon Him) or Moses (Peace Be Upon Him) or liberal values?

Or are we to understand that allowing the original inhabitants of these lands—inside and outside Palestine—whether they are Christian, Muslim or Jew, to determine their fate, runs contrary to principles of democracy, human rights and the teachings of prophets? If not, why is there so much opposition to a referendum?

The newly elected Palestinian administration recently took office. All independent observers have confirmed that this government represents the electorate. Unbelievingly, they have put the elected government under pressure and have advised it to recognize the Israeli regime, abandon the struggle and follow the programs of the previous government.

If the current Palestinian government had run on the above platform, would the Palestinian people have voted for it? Again, can such position taken in opposition to the

Palestinian government be reconciled with the values outlined earlier? The people are also asking, "why are all
UNSC resolutions in condemnation of Israel vetoed?"

Mr. President,

As you are well aware, I live amongst the people and
am in constant contact with them—many people from
around the Middle East manage to contact me as well.
They do not have faith in these dubious policies either.
There is evidence that the people of the region are becoming increasingly angry with such policies.

It is not my intention to pose too many questions, but
I need to refer to other points as well.

Why is it that any technological and scientific achievement reached in the Middle East region is translated into
and portrayed as a threat to the Zionist regime? Is not scientific R&D one of the basic rights of nations?

You are familiar with history. Aside from the Middle
Ages, in what other point in history has scientific and technical progress been a crime? Can the possibility of scientific
achievements being utilized for military purposes be reason
enough to oppose science and technology altogether? If
such a supposition is true, then all scientific disciplines,
including physics, chemistry, mathematics, medicine, engineering, etc., must be opposed.

Lies were told in the Iraqi matter. What was the result?
I have no doubt that telling lies is reprehensible in any culture, and you do not like to be lied to.

Mr. President,

Don't Latin Americans have the right to ask why their elected government are being opposed and coup leaders supported? Or, Why must they constantly be threatened and live in fear?

The people of Africa are hard-working, creative and talented. They can play an important and valuable role in providing for the needs of humanity and contribute to its material and spiritual progress. Poverty and hardship in large parts of Africa are preventing this from happening. Don't they have the right to ask why their enormous wealth—including minerals—is being looted, despite the fact that they need it more than others?

Again, do such actions correspond to the teachings of Christ and the tenets of human rights?

The brave and faithful people of Iran too have many questions and grievances, including: the coup d'etat of 1953 and the subsequent toppling of the legal government of the day, opposition to the Islamic Revolution, transformation of an Embassy into a headquarters supporting the activities of those opposing the Islamic Republic (many thousands of pages of documents corroborate this claim), support for Saddam in the war waged against Iran, the shooting down of the Iranian passenger plane, freezing the assets of the Iranian nation, increasing threats, anger and displeasure vis-à-vis the scientific and nuclear progress of the Iranian nation (just when all Iranians are jubilant and

celebrating their country's progress), and many other grievances that I will not refer to in this letter.

Mr. President,

September Eleven was a horrendous incident. The killing of innocents is deplorable and appalling in any part of
the world. Our government immediately declared its dis-
gust with the perpetrators and offered its condolences to
the bereaved and expressed its sympathies.

All governments have a duty to protect the lives, prop-
erty and good standing of their citizens. Reportedly your
government employs extensive security, protection and
intelligence systems—and even hunts its opponents abroad.
September eleven was not a simple operation. Could it be
planned and executed without coordination with intelligence and security services—or their extensive infiltration?
Of course this is just an educated guess. Why have the various aspects of the attacks been kept secret? Why are we not
told who botched their responsibilities? And, why aren't
those responsible and the guilty parties identified and put
on trial?

All governments have a duty to provide security and
peace of mind for their citizens. For some years now, the
people of your country and neighbors of world trouble
spots do not have peace of mind. After 9/11, instead of
healing and tending to the emotional wounds of the sur-
vivors and the American people—who had been immensely
traumatized by the attacks—some Western media only

intensified the climate of fear and insecurity—some constantly talked about the possibility of new terror attacks and kept the people in fear. Is that service to the American people? Is it possible to calculate the damages incurred from fear and panic?

American citizens lived in constant fear of fresh attacks that could come at any moment and in any place. They felt insecure in the street, in their place of work and at home. Who would be happy with this situation? Why was the media, instead of conveying a feeling of security and providing peace of mind, giving rise to a feeling of insecurity?

Some believe that the hype paved the way—and was the justification—for an attack on Afghanistan. Again I need to refer to the role of media. In media charters, correct dissemination of information and honest reporting of a story are established tenets. I express my deep regret about the disregard shown by certain Western media for these principles. The main pretext for an attack on Iraq was the existence of WMDs. This was repeated incessantly—for the public to finally believe—and the ground set for an attack on Iraq.

Will the truth not be lost in a contrived and deceptive climate? Again, if the truth is allowed to be lost, how can that be reconciled with the earlier mentioned values?

Is the truth known to the Almighty lost as well?

Mr. President,

In countries around the world, citizens provide for the

expenses of governments so that their governments in turn are able to serve them.

The question here is "what has the hundreds of billions of dollars, spent every year to pay for the Iraqi campaign, produced for the citizens?"

As Your Excellency is aware, in some states of your country, people are living in poverty. Many thousands are homeless and unemployment is a huge problem. Of course these problems exist—to a larger or lesser extent—in other countries as well. With these conditions in mind, can the gargantuan expenses of the campaign—paid from the public treasury—be explained and be consistent with the afore-mentioned principles?

What has been said, are some of the grievances of the people around the world, in our region and in your country. But my main contention—which I am hoping you will agree to some of it—is:

Those in power have a specific time in office and do not rule indefinitely, but their names will be recorded in history and will be consistently judged in the immediate and distant futures.

The people will scrutinize our presidencies. Did we manage to bring peace, security and prosperity for the people or insecurity and unemployment?

Did we intend to establish justice or just supported special interest groups, and by forcing many people to live in poverty and hardship made a few people rich and powerful—thus trading the approval of the people and the Almighty with theirs?

Did we defend the rights of the underprivileged or ignore them?

Did we defend the rights of all people around the world or imposed wars on them, interfered illegally in their affairs, established hellish prisons and incarcerated some of them?

Did we bring the world peace and security or raised the specter of intimidation and threats?

Did we tell the truth to our nation and others around the world or presented an inverted version of it?

Were we on the side of people or the occupiers and oppressors?

Did our administrations set out to promote rational behavior, logic, ethics, peace, fulfilling obligations, justice, service to the people, prosperity, progress and respect for human dignity or the force of guns, intimidation, insecurity, disregard for the people, delaying the progress and excellence of other nations, and trample on people's rights?

And finally, they will judge us on whether we remained true to our oath of office—to serve the people, which is our main task, and the traditions of the prophets—or not?

Mr. President,

How much longer can the world tolerate this situation?

Where will this trend lead the world to?

How long must the people of the world pay for the incorrect decisions of some rulers?

How much longer will the specter of insecurity—raised from the stockpiles of weapons of mass destruction—hunt the people of the world?

How much longer will the blood of the innocent men, women and children be spilled on the streets, and people's houses destroyed over their heads?

Are you pleased with the current condition of the world?

Do you think present policies can continue?

If billions of dollars spent on security, military campaigns and troop movement were instead spent on investment and assistance for poor countries, promotion of health, combating different diseases, education and improvement of mental and physical fitness, assistance to the victims of natural disasters, creation of employment opportunities and production, development projects and poverty alleviation, establishment of peace, mediation between disputing states, and extinguishing the flames of racial, ethnic and other conflicts, where would the world be today? Would not your government and people be justifiably proud?

Would not your administration's political and economic standing have been stronger?

And I am most sorry to say, would there have been an ever increasing global hatred of the American government?

Mr. President, it is not my intention to distress anyone.

If Prophet Abraham, Isaac, Jacob, Ishmael, Joseph, or

Jesus Christ (Peace Be Upon Him) were with us today, how would they have judged such behavior? Will we be given a role to play in the promised world, where justice will become universal and Jesus Christ (Peace Be Upon Him) will be present? Will they even accept us?

My basic question is this: Is there no better way to interact with the rest of the world? Today there are hundreds of millions of Christians, hundreds of millions of Muslims and millions of people who follow the teachings of Moses (Peace Be Upon Him). All divine religions share and respect one word and that is "monotheism" or belief in a single God and no other in the world.

The Holy Koran stresses this common word and calls on all followers of divine religions and says: (3.64) Say: O followers of the Book! come to an equitable proposition between us and you that we shall not serve any but Allah and (that) we shall not associate aught with Him, and (that) some of us shall not take others for lords besides Allah; but if they turn back, then say: Bear witness that we are Muslims. (The Family of Imran)

Mr. President,

According to divine verses, we have all been called upon to worship one God and follow the teachings of divine Prophets.

"To worship a God which is above all powers in the world and can do all He pleases." "The Lord which knows that which is hidden and visible, the past and the future, knows what goes on in the Hearts of His servants and records their deeds."

"The Lord who is the possessor of the heavens and the earth and all universe is His court" "planning for the universe is done by His hands, and gives His servants the glad tidings of mercy and forgiveness of sins." "He is the companion of the oppressed and the enemy of oppressors." "He is the Compassionate, the Merciful." "He is the recourse of the faithful and guides them towards the light from darkness." "He is witness to the actions of His servants." "He calls on servants to be faithful and do good deeds, and asks them to stay on the path of righteousness and remain steadfast." "Calls on servants to heed His prophets and He is a witness to their deeds." "A bad ending belongs only to those who have chosen the life of this world and disobey Him and oppress His servants." And "A good land and eternal paradise belong to those servants who fear His majesty and do not follow their lascivious selves."

We believe a return to the teachings of the divine prophets is the only road leading to salvation and have been told that Your Excellency follows the teachings of Jesus (Peace Be Upon Him) and believes in the divine promise of the rule of the righteous on Earth.

We also believe that Jesus Christ (Peace Be Upon Him) was one of the great prophets of the Almighty. He has been repeatedly praised in the Koran. Jesus (Peace Be Upon Him) has been quoted in Koran as well: (19.36) And surely

Allah is my Lord and your Lord, therefore serve Him; this is the right path.

Service to and obedience of the Almighty is the credo of all divine messengers.

The God of all people in Europe, Asia, Africa, America, the Pacific and the rest of the world is one. He is the Almighty who wants to guide and give dignity to all His servants. He has given greatness to Humans.

We again read in the Holy Book: "The Almighty God sent His prophets with miracles and clear signs to guide the people and show them divine signs and purify them from sins and pollutions. And He sent the Book and the balance so that the people display justice and avoid the rebellious."

All of the above verses can be seen, one way or the other, in the Good Book as well.

Divine prophets have promised:

The day will come when all humans will congregate before the court of the Almighty, so that their deeds are examined. The good will be directed towards Heaven and evildoers will meet divine retribution. I trust both of us believe in such a day, but it will not be easy to calculate the actions of rulers, because we must be answerable to our nation and all others whose lives have been directly or indirectly affected by our actions.

All prophets speak of peace and tranquility for man—based on monotheism, justice and respect for human dignity.

Do you not think that if all of us come to believe in and abide by these principles, that is, monotheism, worship of God, justice, respect for the dignity of man, belief in the Last Day, we can overcome the present problems of the world—that are the result of disobedience to the Almighty and the teachings of prophets—and improve our performance?

Do you not think that belief in these principles promotes and guarantees peace, friendship and justice?

Do you not think that the aforementioned written or unwritten principles are universally represented?

Will you not accept this invitation? That is, a genuine return to the teachings of prophets, to monotheism and justice, to preserve human dignity and obedience to the Almighty and His prophets?

Mr. President,

History tells us that repressive and cruel governments do not survive. God has entrusted the fate of men to them. The Almighty has not left the universe and humanity to their own devices. Many things have happened contrary to the wishes and plans of governments. These tell us that there is a higher power at work and all events are determined by Him.

Can one deny the signs of change in the world today?

Is the situation of the world today comparable to that of 10 years ago? Changes happen fast and come at a furious pace.

The people of the world are not happy with the status quo and pay little heed to the promises and comments made by a number of influential world leaders. Many people around the world feel insecure and oppose the spreading of insecurity and war and do not approve of and accept dubious policies.

The people are protesting the increasing gap between the haves and the have-nots and the rich and poor countries.

The people are disgusted with increasing corruption.

The people of many countries are angry about the attacks on their cultural foundations and the disintegration of families. They are equally dismayed with the fading of care and compassion. The people of the world have no faith in international organizations, because their rights are not advocated by these organizations.

Liberalism and Western-style democracy have not been able to help realize the ideals of humanity. Today these two concepts have failed. Those with insight can already hear the sounds of the shattering and fall of the ideology and thoughts of the Liberal democratic systems.

We increasingly see that people around the world are flocking towards a main focal point—that is the Almighty God. Undoubtedly through faith in God and the teachings of the prophets, the people will conquer their problems. My question for you is: "Do you not want to join them?"

Mr. President,

Whether you like it or not, the world is gravitating

towards faith in the Almighty and justice and the will of God will prevail over all things.

Vasalam Ala Man Ataba'al hoda

Mahmood Ahmadi-Najad

President of the Islamic Republic of Iran

Notes

Chapter 1

1. "Iran urges worldwide Islamic revolt," *Iran News Daily,* June 30, 2005, www.irannewsdaily.com/v2/view_news.asp?id=119359, quoted in Kenneth R. Timmerman, *Countdown to Crisis: The Coming Nuclear Showdown with Iran,* updated ed. (New York: Three Rivers Press, 2006), 322.

2. Bridget Johnson, "Most dangerous man forging alliances on our doorstep," Daily News of Los Angeles, January 15, 2007, www.dailynews.com/bridgetjohnson/ci_5018937.

3. *What Makes Iran Tick: Islamist Ideology and Hegemonic Interests* (Washington, DC: Iran Policy Committee, 2006), xii.

4. Yossi Melman and Meir Javedanfar, *The Nuclear Sphinx of Tehran: Mahmoud Ahmadinejad and the State of Iran* (New York: Carroll & Graf Publishers, 2007), 42–43.

5. Johnson, "Most dangerous man," January 15, 2007.

6. Omar Fadhil, "Is Hezbollah launching Iran's Armageddon," Iran Defence Forum, August 4, 2006, www.irandefence.net/show threadphp?t=1980.

7. *What Makes Tehran Tick,* 97–98.

8. Mortimer B. Zuckerman, "Finishing the job," *U.S. News & World Report,* July 31, 2006, 68.

9. *What Makes Tehran Tick,* 46.

10. *What Makes Tehran Tick,* 81.

11. *What Makes Tehran Tick,* 29.

12. "Ahmadinejad's latest: 'Satan inspires Bush,'" WorldNetDaily, October 26, 2006, www.worldnetdaily.com/news/article.asp? ARTICLE_ID=52476.

13. "Iran: Britain, allies 'arrogant' for no apology," Associated Press, April 1, 2007, www.newsday.com/news/nationworld/world/ny-woiran015154218apr01,0,2440023,p.

14. "British expect Iran to begin release of 15 captive sailors, marines 'within hours,'" Fox News, April 4, 2007, www.foxnews.com/story/0,2933,263924,00.html.

15. "Chavez cements Iran ties with Tehran visit," CNN, July 28, 2006, http://edition.cnn.com/2006/WORLD/americas/07/28/chavez.iran.reut/.

16. Johnson, "Most dangerous man," January 15, 2007.

17. *What Makes Tehran Tick,* 79.

18. *What Makes Tehran Tick,* 31–32.

19. Joel Rosenberg, January 2, 2007, www.joelrosenberg.com.

20. Timmerman, *Countdown to Crisis,* 326.

21. *What Makes Tehran Tick,* 113.

22. Ed Blanche, "Claws of the bear," *Middle East* (April 2007), 6.

23. *What Makes Tehran Tick,* 32.

24. Wilhelm Gesenius, *Gesenius' Hebrew-Chaldee Lexicon to the Old Testament* (Reprint, Grand Rapids: Eerdmans,1949), 752. For an extensive, thorough presentation of the grammatical and philological support for taking Rosh as a place name, see James D. Price, "Rosh: An Ancient Land Known to Ezekiel," *Grace Theological Journal* 6 (1985): 67–89, 82; Clyde E. Billington Jr., "The Rosh People in History and Prophecy (Part Two)," *Michigan Theological Journal* 3 (1992): 66–67; Clyde E. Billington Jr., "The Rosh People in History and Prophecy (Part Three)," *Michigan Theological Journal* 4 (1993): 59, 61; Jon Mark Ruthven, *The Prophecy That Is Shaping History: New Research on Ezekiel's Vision of the End* (Fairfax, VA: Xulon Press, 2003); and Gesenius, *Lexicon,* 752. In his original Latin version of the lexicon titled *Thesaurus Linguae Hebraeae et Chaldaeae Veteris Testamenti,* Gesenius has nearly one page of notes dealing with the word *Rosh* and the Rosh people mentioned in Ezekiel 38–39. This page of notes does not appear in any of the English translations of Gesenius's lexicon. Those who disagree with Gesenius have failed to refute his sizable body of convincing evidence identifying Rosh with Russia.

Chapter 2

1. Ali M. Ansari, *Confronting Iran: The Failure of American Foreign Policy and the Next Great Crisis in the Middle East* (New York: Basic Books, 2006), 226.

2. The main sources for much of the biographical information I've included are Alireza Jafarzadeh, *The Iran Threat: President Ahmadinejad and the Coming Nuclear Crisis* (New York: Palgrave, 2007), 1–35, and Yossi Melman and Meir Javedanfar, *The Nuclear Sphinx of Tehran: Mahmoud Ahmadinejad and the State of Iran* (New York: Carroll & Graf, 2007), 1–40.

3. Jafarzadeh, *The Iran Threat,* 3–4.

4. Jafarzadeh, *The Iran Threat,* 5.

5. Jafarzadeh, *The Iran Threat,* 5.

6. Melman and Javedanfar, *The Nuclear Sphinx of Tehran,* xi.

7. "Mahoud Ahmadinejad," Fox News, January 10, 2007, www .globalsecurity.org/military/world/iran/ahmadinejad.htm.

8. Jafarzadeh, *The Iran Threat,* 12.

9. "Hostage Roeder: 'Ahmadinejad threatened to kidnap my son,'" Spiegel Online International, June 30, 2005, www.spiegel.de/ international/0,1518,363072,00.html; Kenneth R. Timmerman, *Countdown to Crisis,* updated ed. (New York: Three Rivers Press, 2006), 320–21.

10. "Mahoud Ahmadinejad," Fox News, January 10, 2007, www.fox news.com

11. Jafarzadeh, *The Iran Threat,* 19.

12. Jafarzadeh, *The Iran Threat,* 19.

13. Jafarzadeh, *The Iran Threat,* 23.

14. Jafarzadeh, *The Iran Threat,* 23.

15. Fouad Ajami, "Maintaining perspective," *U.S. News & World Report,* March 5, 2007, 49.

16. Ali Akbar Dareini, "Iran's discontent with Ahmadinejad grows," Associated Press, January 17, 2007, http://seattlepi.nwsource.com/ national/1107AP_Iran_Ahmadinejad_Woes.html.

17. Ewen MacAskill and Simon Tisdall, "Ahmadinejad has 70% approval rating," *Guardian,* June 22, 2006, www.guardian.co.uk/iran/story/0,,1801867,00.html.

18. Robert Tait, "President's future in doubt as MPs rebel and economic crisis grows," *Guardian,* January 17, 2007, www.guardian.co.uk/frontpage/story/0,,1991414,00.html; Frances Harrison, "Growing pressures on Ahmadinejad," BBC News, January 16, 2007, http://news.bbc.co.uk/2/hi/middle_east/6267105.stm.

19. Ian Bremmer, "A useful distraction: why the Iranian mullahs will never silence Mahmoud Ahmadinejad," Slate, April 16, 2007, www.slate.com/id/2164237.

Chapter 3

1. Anton La Guardia, "'Divine mission' driving Iran's new leader," Telegraph Media Group, January 15, 2006, telegraph.co.uk.

2. Daniel Pipes, "The mystical menace of Mahmoud Ahmadinejad," *New York Sun,* January 10, 2006, www.danielpipes.org/article/3258.

3. Yossi Melman and Meir Javedanfar, *The Nuclear Sphinx of Tehran: Mahmoud Ahmadinejad and the State of Iran* (New York: Carroll & Graf, 2007), 46.

4. Mohsen Sazegara, "Islam's second revolution," www.sazegara.net/english/archives/2005/11/the_second_isla.html.

5. Melman and Javedanfar, *The Nuclear Sphinx of Tehran,* 56.

6. Neil MacFarquhar, "Iraq's shadow widens Sunni-Shiite split in U.S.," *New York Times,* February 4, 2007.

7. MacFarquhar, "Iraq's shadow widens."

8. Bobby Ghosh, "Why they hate each other," *Time,* March 5, 2007, 32.

9. John L. Esposito, *What Everyone Needs to Know About Islam* (New York: Oxford University, 2002), 183. For Sunni Muslims the term *imam* is much broader. It refers to any "prayer leader and person who delivers the Friday sermon."

10. Esposito, *What Everyone Needs to Know About Islam,* 48.

11. There are many, often contradictory, versions of the traditions related to the Hidden Imam. The version I have followed is the

one most often presented in popular books. Moojan Momen, *An Introduction to Shi'i Islam: The History and Doctrines of Twelver Shi'ism* (New Haven: Yale University, 1985), 159.

12. Momen, *An Introduction to Shi'i Islam*, 161.
13. Esposito, *What Everyone Needs to Know About Islam*, 49.
14. Momen, *An Introduction to Shi'i Islam*, 165.
15. Momen, *An Introduction to Shi'i Islam*, 161–62.
16. Momen, *An Introduction to Shi'i Islam*, 162.
17. Momen, *An Introduction to Shi'i Islam*, 165.
18. Momen, *An Introduction to Shi'i Islam*, 166.
19. Esposito, *What Everyone Needs to Know About Islam*, 49.
20. "Iran leader's U.N. finale reveals apocalyptic view," WorldNet-Daily, September 21, 2006, www.worldnetdaily.com/news/article.asp?ARTICLE_ID=52071.
21. Melman and Javedanfar, *The Nuclear Sphinx of Tehran*, 51.
22. Melman and Javedanfar, *The Nuclear Sphinx of Tehran*, 46.
23. Vali Nasr, *The Shia Revival: How Conflicts Within Islam Will Shape the Future* (New York: W. W. Norton, 2006), 220.
24. Scott Peterson, "Waiting for the Rapture in Iran," *Christian Science Monitor*, December 21, 2005, www.csmonitor.com/2005/1221/p01s04-wome.html.
25. Pepe Escobar, "The ultimate martyr," Asia Times Online, May 31, 2006, www.atimes.com.
26. Melman and Javedanfar, *The Nuclear Sphinx of Tehran*, 46.
27. Melman and Javedanfar, *The Nuclear Sphinx of Tehran*, 46.
28. Escobar, "The ultimate martyr," May 31, 2006.
29. "Jesus, Mahdi both coming, says Iran's Ahmadinejad," WorldNet-Daily, December 19, 2006, www.worldnetdaily.com/news/article.asp?ARTICLE_ID=53430.
30. La Guardia, " 'Divine mission' driving Iran's new leader," January 15, 2006.
31. "Iran prepares people for 'Messiah miracles,'" WorldNetDaily, February 2, 2007, www.worldnetdaily/com/news/article.asp?ARTICLE_ID=53964.

32. "Iran website heralding 'Mahdi' by springtime," WorldNetDaily, January 16, 2007, www.worldnetdaily.com/news/article.asp? ARTICLE_ID=53577.

33. Ed Blanche, "The shark, the crocodile and the 'silent coup,'" *Middle East* (February 2007), 20.

34. Blanche, "The shark, the crocodile and the 'silent coup,'" 20.

35. Melman and Javedanfar, *The Nuclear Sphinx of Tehran*, 45.

36. Kenneth R. Timmerman, *Countdown to Crisis: The Coming Nuclear Showdown with Iran*, updated ed. (New York: Three Rivers Press, 2006), 326.

37. Melman and Javedanfar, *The Nuclear Sphinx of Tehran*, 50–51.

38. Raymond Whitaker, "Mahmoud Ahmadinejad: The nuclear prophet," *Independent*, January 15, 2006, http://news.independent .co.uk/people/profiles/article338625.ece.

39. Nasr, *The Shia Revival*, 133–34.

40. Timmerman, *Countdown to Crisis*, 327.

41. *What Makes Iran Tick: Islamist Ideology and Hegemonic Interests* (Washington, DC: Iran Policy Committee, 2006), 113.

42. Timmerman, *Countdown to Crisis*, 326.

43. Blanche, "The shark, the crocodile and the 'silent coup,'" 23.

44. Melman and Javedanfar, *The Nuclear Sphinx of Tehran*, 46.

45. Melman and Javedanfar, *The Nuclear Sphinx of Tehran*, 46.

46. Timmerman, *Countdown to Crisis*, 326.

47. Melman and Javedanfar, *The Nuclear Sphinx of Tehran*, 49.

48. Melman and Javedanfar, *The Nuclear Sphinx of Tehran*, 49.

49. Momen, *An Introduction to Shi'i Islam*, 166.

50. Melman and Javedanfar, *The Nuclear Sphinx of Tehran*, 43–44.

51. Melman and Javedanfar, *The Nuclear Sphinx of Tehran*, 44; Momen, *An Introduction to Shi'i Islam*, 166.

52. Momen, *An Introduction to Shi'i Islam*, 166.

53. Khaled Farhan, "Iraqi cult leader killed in Najaf battle," Yahoo News, January 29, 2007, http://news.yahoo.com/s/nm/ 20070129/ts_nm/iraq_dc_84.

54. Babak Dehghanpisheh, "Apocalypse now," *Newsweek*, February 12, 2007, 36–37.

55. Melman and Javedanfar, *The Nuclear Sphinx of Tehran,* 57.

56. Melman and Javedanfar, *The Nuclear Sphinx of Tehran,* 57.

57. *Middle East Media Research Institute,* April 22, 2005, no. 897.

58. *Middle East Media Research Institute,* April 22, 2005, no. 897.

59. Joel Rosenberg, "Iran sobered us up on New Year's," National Review Online, January 3, 2007, http://article.nationalreview .com/?q=Nzc1YTNjZDlmZjU3MzBjMTNhMjFhNDNmYj NmNjU0NTI=.

60. Joel C. Rosenberg, "Mesmerized media," National Review Online, September 20, 2006, http://article.nationalreview .com/?q=Zjg2MjgxZmVkNDkxOGZiN2RiMWNiZjUw YjhjOTMxZWU=.

Chapter 4

1. Yigal Carmon, "The role of holocaust denial in the ideology and strategy of the Iranian regime," *Middle East Media Research Institute,* December 15, 2006, no. 307, http://memri.org/bin/opener .cgi?Page=archives&ID=IA30706.

2. Kenneth R. Timmerman, *Countdown to Crisis: The Coming Nuclear Showdown with Iran,* updated ed. (New York: Three Rivers Press, 2006), 320.

3. Timmerman, *Countdown to Crisis,* 320.

4. Quotes not indicated as otherwise are from "Iran's president Mahmoud Ahmadinejad in his own words," Anti-Defamation League, June 3, 2007, www.adl.org/main_Anti_Semitism_International/ ahmadinejad_words.htm.

5. "Ahmadinejad: countdown to Israel's destruction has begun," Ynetnews, June 3, 2007, www.ynetnews.com/articles/0,73 40,L-3407915,00.html.

6. "Iran to 'cut off hand' of foes," Al Jazeera English, April 18, 2007, http://english.aljazeera.net/NR/exeres/08D92123-E910-4E BA-AE1D-DEFFB1581928.htm.

7. "Ahmadinejad in Sudan: 'Zionists are the true manifestation of Satan,'" *Haaretz,* March 1, 2007, www.haaretz.com/hasen/spages/ 832229.html.

8. Lynn Vincent, "Sailing into harm's way," *World,* February 3, 2007, 19.

9. *Middle East Media Research Institute,* October 27, 2006, no. 1337.

10. *Middle East Media Research Institute,* December 15, 2006, no. 307.

11. "Ahmadinejad's latest: 'Satan inspires Bush,'" WorldNetDaily, October 16, 2006, www.worldnetdaily.com/news/article .asp?ARTICLE_ID=52476.

12. Con Coughlin, "Ready for war," Telegraph Media Group, February 25, 2007, telegraph.co.uk.

13. Aaron Klein, "Former Mossad chief: assassinate Ahmadinejad," Ynetnews, February 14, 2007.

14. Carmon, "The role of Holocaust denial," *Middle East Media Research Institute,* December 15, 2006.

15. Carmon, "The role of Holocaust denial," *Middle East Media Research Institute,* December 15, 2006.

16. Carmon, "The role of Holocaust denial," *Middle East Media Research Institute,* December 15, 2006.

17. Carmon, "The role of Holocaust denial," *Middle East Media Research Institute,* December 15, 2006.

18. Yossi Melman and Meir Javedanfar, *The Nuclear Sphinx of Tehran: Mahmoud Ahmadinejad and the State of Iran* (New York: Carroll & Graf, 2007), 53.

19. "KKK's David Duke tells Iran Holocaust Conference that gas chambers not used to kill Jews," Fox News, December 13, 2006, www.foxnews.com/story/0,2933,236014,00.html.

20. *Middle East Media Research Institute,* no. 1443, January 30, 2007.

21. *Middle East Media Research Institute,* no. 1566, May 2, 2007.

22. *Middle East Media Research Institute,* no. 1337, October 27, 2006.

23. "Iran's President Mahmoud Ahmadinejad in his own words," Anti-Defamation League, February 28, 2007, www.adl.org/main_Anti_ Semitism_International/ahmadinejad_words.htm.

24. Walter R. Newell, "Why Ahmadinejad is smiling," Weekly Standard.com, October 16, 2006, www.weeklystandard.com/ Content/Public/Articles/000/000/012/795hlmvk.asp.

25. "In case you missed it: transcript of the interview with Mahmoud Ahmadinejad," Vital Perspective, http://vitalperspective.typepad .com/vital_perspective_clarity/2006/08/in_case_you_mis.html.

26. "Netanyahu moves to put Ahmadinejad on trial," Ynetnews, January 26, 2007, http://web.israelinsider.com/Articles/ Politics/10471.htm.

27. Hagit Klaiman, "Netanyahu in London: Ahmadinejad must be tried in Hague," Ynetnews, January 26, 2007 www.ynetnews.com.

28. *What Makes Iran Tick: Islamist Ideology and Hegemonic Interests* (Washington, DC: Iran Policy Committee, 2006), 101.

29. "Germany likens Ahmadinejad to Hitler," Gulf News, February 4, 2006, http://archive.gulfnews.com/indepth/irancrisis/more_stories/ 10016391.html.

30. "Newt Gingrich: Iran's President is the new Hitler," Newsmax, January 25, 2006, www.newsmax.com/archives/ic/2006/1/25/ 100038.shtml.

31. Newell, "Why Ahmadinejad is smiling," *Weekly Standard*, October 16, 2006. www.weeklystandard.com.

Chapter 5

1. *Bulletin of the Atomic Scientists*, January–February 2007.

2. *Bulletin of the Atomic Scientists*, January–February 2007, 66.

3. *Bulletin of the Atomic Scientists*, January–February 2007, 66.

4. *Bulletin of the Atomic Scientists*, January–February 2007, 26.

5. *Bulletin of the Atomic Scientists*, January–February 2007, 28.

6. *Bulletin of the Atomic Scientists*, January–February 2007, 31.

7. *Bulletin of the Atomic Scientists*, January–February 2007, 33.

8. *Bulletin of the Atomic Scientists*, January–February 2007, 33.

9. Alireza Jafarzadeh, *The Iran Threat: President Ahmadinejad and the Coming Nuclear Crisis* (New York: Palgrave, 2007), 208.

10. David E. Sanger, "Atomic agency concludes Iran is stepping up nuclear work," *New York Times*, May 14, 2007, www.nytimes.com/ 2007/05/14/world/middleeast/14cnd-iran.html?ei=5065&en= 3c9eea7cdf75deb3&ex=117980.

11. This information is from *What Makes Iran Tick: Islamist Ideology and Hegemonic Interests* (Washington, DC: Iran Policy Committee, 2006), 60–61.

12. Jafarzadeh, *The Iran Threat,* 188.

13. Jafarzadeh, *The Iran Threat,* 190.

14. Jafarzadeh, *The Iran Threat,* 191.

15. *What Makes Tehran Tick,* 12.

16. Jafarzadeh, *The Iran Threat,* 197.

17. Jafarzadeh, *The Iran Threat,* 197.

18. *What Makes Tehran Tick,* 116–117.

19. "Iran goes nuclear, joins elite club: Ahmadinejad," *Hindu,* April 9, 2007, www.hindu.com/thehindu/holnus/003200704092321 .htm.

20. "Iran goes nuclear" *Hindu,* April 9, 2007.

21. Nazila Fathi, "Iran says it can enrich uranium," *New York Times,* April 10, 2007.

22. "Ceremony to mark 'National Day for Nuclear Technology' begins," Presidency of the Islamic Republic of Iran, April 10, 2007, www.president.ir/en/view.php?ArtID=3666.

23. "Iran vows nuclear expansion," *Gulf Daily News,* April 10, 2007, www.gulf-daily-news.com/printnews.asp?Article=177309.

24. Fathi, "Iran says it can enrich uranium," *New York Times,* April 10, 2007.

25. Fathi, "Iran says it can enrich uranium," *New York Times,* April 10, 2007.

26. Unless otherwise indicated, the source for these statements is Jafarzadeh, *The Iran Threat,* 190–97.

27. "Ahmadinejad vows Iran will 'resist to the end.'" *Forbes,* April 16, 2007 www.forbes.com.

28. Nasser Karimi, "Iran: sanctions could push nuclear drive," Associated Press, April 16, 2007, www.iranfocus.com/modules/news/ article.php?storyid=10885.

29. "Ahmadinejad says Iran ready for 'final nuclear step,'" Breitbart, November 16, 2006, www.breitbart.com/news/2006/11/16/ 061116161903.erpjjyqw.html.

30. Alireza Jafarzadeh, "In Iran, train with 'no brakes' about to hit Ahmadinejad," Fox News, March 4, 2007, www.foxnews.com/story/0,2933,255531,00.html.

31. Parisa Hafezi, "Iran won't back down in atom row—president," Star Online, April 24, 2007, http://thestar.com.my/news/story.asp?file=/2007/4/24/worldupdates/2007-04-24T0217 30Z_01_NOOTR_RTRJONC_0_-295344-3&sec=World updates.

32. *Middle East Media Research Institute,* February 28, 2007, no. 1478. The cartoon can be viewed at www.memritv.org/search.asp?ACT= S9&P1=1390.

33. "Timeline: Iran's nuclear program," CNN, April 9, 2007, http://cnn.worldnews.printthis.clickability.com/pt/cpt?action=cpt&title= Timeline%3A+Iran.

34. Ed Blanche, "Iran eyes 'the high ground,' " *Middle East,* April 2007, 22–23.

35. "Ahmadinejad: supreme leader decides Iran's nuclear policy," Iran Focus, February 1, 2007 www.iranfocus.com.

36. Blanche, "The shark, the crocodile and the 'silent coup,' " 23.

37. "Ahmadinejad: supreme leader decides Iran's nuclear policy," Iran Focus, February 1, 2007 www.iranfocus.com.

38. Jafarzadeh, *The Iran Threat,* 198.

39. Jafarzadeh, *The Iran Threat,* 198.

40. The sources for the information about the atomic banknotes are "Iran defiant with atomic banknote," BBC News, March 12, 2007, http://news.bbc.co.uk/go/pr/fr/-/2/hi/middle_east/6441777.stm; "In snub to UN sanctions, Iran introduces atomic banknotes," Iran Focus, March 12, 2007, www.iranfocus.com/modules/news/article.php?storyid=10423; "World must act to stop Ahmadinejad," *Jerusalem Post,* March 10, 2007, www.jpost.com/servlet.Satellite? cid=1173173977498&pagename=JPost%2FJPArtic.

41. Gregory Viscusi, "ElBaradei says Iran is at least 5 years away from nuclear arms," Bloomberg, January 26, 2007, www.bloomberg.com.

42. Con Coughlin, "Israel seeks all clear for Iran air strike," Telegraph Media Group, February 25, 2007, telegraph.co.uk.

43. Coughlin, "Israel seeks all clear," February 25, 2007.
44. Kenneth M. Pollack, *The Persian Puzzle* (New York: Random House, 2005), 388.

Chapter 6

1. The biblical, eschatological viewpoint presented in this book is commonly known as premillennial-pretribulationism, or more specifically, dispensationalism. Premillennialism means that Jesus will return before (pre) a literal one-thousand-year reign on a renewed, restored earth (Revelation 20:1–6). Pretribulationism teaches that the Rapture, or snatching away, of living believers, taught in 1 Thessalonians 4:17, will occur before the onset of the future seven-year tribulation period. Clearly, not all Christians agree on the specific events of the end times. However, all true Christians do believe in a literal, visible, personal return of Jesus Christ at the end of the age to judge the living and the dead. For a basic presentation of the various views and a more in-depth presentation of the premillennian-pretribulation position, see Mark Hitchcock, *The Complete Book of Bible Prophecy* (Wheaton: Tyndale House Publishers, 1999), 27–48.
2. This information and illustration are originally from Peter Stoner, who is referenced by Josh McDowell in his classic, *Evidence That Demands a Verdict* (see www.bible-prophecy.com/fulfilled.htm).
3. "Iran could join CSTO—Bordyuzha," Interfax, May 14, 2007, www.interfax.ru/e/B/politics/28.html?id_issue=11741564.

Chapter 7

1. Lynn Vincent, "Acceptable targets," *World,* April 21, 2007, 28.
2. *Newsweek,* November 1, 1999.

Appendix A

1. The transcript of the speech is from Iran Focus, October 28, 2005, www.iranfocus.com/modules/news/article.php?storyid=4146.